PEACE IN EUROPE

The Royal Institute of International Affairs is an unofficial body which promotes the scientific study of international questions and does not express opinions of its own. The opinions expressed in this publication are the responsibility of the author.

The Institute gratefully acknowledges the comments and suggestions of the following who read the manuscript on behalf of the Research Committee: Alan Bullock, Roger Morgan, and Kenneth Younger.

PEACE IN EUROPE

East-West Relations 1966–1968 and the
Prospects for a European Settlement

Karl E. Birnbaum

Director of the Swedish Institute of International Affairs

*Written under the auspices of the
Harvard Center for International Affairs and published
in co-operation with the Royal Institute
of International Affairs*

OXFORD UNIVERSITY PRESS
LONDON   OXFORD   NEW YORK
1970

Oxford University Press

LONDON   OXFORD   NEW YORK

GLASGOW   TORONTO   MELBOURNE   WELLINGTON

CAPE TOWN   SALISBURY   IBADAN   NAIROBI   LUSAKA   DAR ES SALAAM   ADDIS ABABA

BOMBAY   CALCUTTA   MADRAS   KARACHI   LAHORE   DACCA

KUALA LUMPUR   SINGAPORE   HONG KONG   TOKYO

First published as an Oxford University Press paperback
by Oxford University Press, London, 1970

Printed in Great Britain by
The Eastern Press Limited, London and Reading

To my father
Immanuel Birnbaum
who has worked devotedly for
half a century to promote a
better understanding between
Eastern and Western Europe

CONTENTS

PREFACE

A STUDY based mainly on public official statements has obvious pitfalls. It may be an exaggeration to claim that history is what does *not* appear in the records, but it is certainly true that official documents are at best an imperfect reflection of how those in power think and feel, and how they see the world around them. An analyst who attempts to review and interpret official statements must therefore complement such material with other sources of information. These can be best acquired through contact with persons sufficiently near the centres of policy-making to understand their intricate workings yet free enough to comment on the findings and observations of those who have set themselves the task of scrutinizing what these centres disgorge. I have been most fortunate in being able to enlist the help of a great number of thoughtful people in such positions—many of them personal friends—at all stages in the preparation of the present study.

From the very outset I could draw on the experience and insight of several European scholars and writers in both East and West who gave me valuable assistance in identifying relevant documents and putting them into their proper context. Those who helped me in this way included László Báti, Budapest; Marian Dobrosielski, Warsaw; Niels J. Haagerup, Copenhagen; Herbert Kröger, Potsdam; Ladislav Líska, Prague; Eberhard Schulz, Bonn; and Jacques Vernant, Paris.

I was invited to join the Center for International Affairs at Harvard University for the academic year 1967–8 as a research associate. For this invitation and the financial support that went with it, I am deeply indebted to Henry Kissinger and Marshall Shulman as well as to the Center's directors during my stay, Robert Bowie and Raymond Vernon. The Center proved a congenial and most stimulating environment for work. Its librarians gave me very efficient assistance in locating the relevant material among Harvard's imposing and bewildering multitude of book collections. The Russian Research Center at the University was also an excellent aid, and I am grateful to Abram Bergson, its director, for allowing me to use its resources.

A number of other institutions have supported this project. A generous grant from the Bank of Sweden Tercentenary Fund made my stay at Harvard possible, and enabled me to employ an assistant at the crucial finishing stage in my work. In the summer of 1968 I spent six weeks at the Institute for Strategic Studies in London, which provided a friendly setting for useful discussions of European security problems, a subject of special concern to the Institute at that time. I wish to thank Alastair Buchan, who was then its director, for this arrangement. I should also like to express my gratitude to the Royal Institute of International Affairs, and especially to Rena Fenteman and Roger Morgan for their unsparing efforts in connection with the publication of this book. Last but not least, my thanks are due to the Board of the Swedish Institute of International Affairs for granting me extended leave of absence from the position of director of the Institute.

I have profited from presenting papers relevant to some sections of this book at three conferences organized in 1968 by the Atlantic Institute in Paris, the Graduate Institute of International Studies at Geneva, and the Institute for Strategic Studies in London.

Two review sessions of early drafts of the manuscript were arranged in the spring of 1969 by Linda Miller at Harvard University and Warner Schilling at Columbia University. To them and to all those who contributed to the fruitful exchange of ideas which took place I extend my warm thanks. In addition, a significant number of people have read and commented on parts or the whole of the manuscript—Peter Bender, Benjamin Brown, Zbigniew Brzezinski, Alastair Buchan, Stanley Hoffmann, Karl Kaiser, Henry Kissinger, Karol Lapter, Richard Löwenthal, Linda Miller, Roger Morgan, Willie Morris, Josef Sego, Marshall Shulman, Walther Stützle, Wolfgang Wagner, and Gerhard Wettig. Their comments helped me to eliminate errors and induced me to reconsider certain points in the light of new evidence. Although I benefited greatly from their criticism I alone am responsible for the end result.

I owe a special debt of gratitude to Donald Bayne Lavery, who has worked with me during the last hectic year. He has not only given me most significant help in carrying out the normal tasks of a research assistant but has also rendered invaluable assistance in forcing me to clarify my own thoughts by relentlessly questioning the seemingly obvious and with a most unusual combination of patience, stubbornness, and good humour. I very much appreciated the diligence of Jacqueline Ahlström who typed the manuscript and sacrificed many beautiful summer days in the process.

A book-writing father is a burden to a family: the larger the family, the greater the burden. I am grateful to Britta, Maria, Anja, Camilla, and Daniel for bearing it with such sympathy and understanding.

Stockholm   K. E. B.

October 1969.

ABBREVIATIONS

CDU/CSU	Christlich Demokratische Union/Christlich-Soziale Union (Christian Democrats and their Bavarian wing, the Christian Social Union)
COMECON	Council for Mutual Economic Aid
CPCS	Communist Party of Czechoslovakia
CPSU	Communist Party of the Soviet Union
EEC	European Economic Community
ESC	European Security Conference
FDP	Freie Demokratische Partei (Free Democrats)
FRG	Federal Republic of Germany
GDR	German Democratic Republic
NATO	North Atlantic Treaty Organization
SALT	Strategic arms limitation talks
SED	Sozialistische Einheitspartei Deutschlands (Socialist Unity Party of Germany—Communist)
SPD	Sozialdemokratische Partei Deutschlands (Social Democrats)
WEU	Western European Union
WTO	Warsaw Treaty Organization

INTRODUCTION

THIS study was conceived and begun in 1966, at a time when the relaxation of tension in Europe seemed to open up possibilities for a more satisfactory *modus vivendi* between East and West, and ultimately for a European settlement. The manuscript was finished in the sombre atmosphere of the months following the invasion of Czechoslovakia in August 1968. Although inevitably the author's general perspective has not been unaffected by the change in the international situation, the basic rationale for the specific approach applied in the book has remained unaltered. From its inception it was planned as an investigation of official thinking in East and West about the more fluid East–West constellation in Europe of the late 1960s, its immediate policy requirements, and long-range potentialities.

For several reasons this comparatively tedious undertaking seemed to be worth while and indeed urgent. The first was my impression that widely prevailing notions about ' the end of the cold war ' and speculations about new European configurations, which characterized public and academic debates in both East and West during 1966–7, tended to underrate the inertia of official thinking in both camps. A realistic assessment of the scope for East–West agreements therefore seemed to call for an analysis of official views. In addition, I felt that a study of this kind might lead to valid conclusions about the priorities and goals of the governing élites in the main centres of decision and thus contribute to an understanding of the process of interaction in East–West relations.

The relaxation of tension in Europe in the mid-1960s was born of the new sense of security following the first nuclear confrontation between the United States and the Soviet Union during the Cuban crisis in October 1962, the termination of the second Berlin crisis, and the emergence of a distinctly limited, yet clearly visible, community of interests between Washington and Moscow to keep their conflict within manageable bounds. The growth of contacts and co-operation between

1

individual countries in Western and Eastern Europe was a
natural consequence of this change in climate and perspective.
In the course of 1963 and 1964 there were indications that the
Soviet leadership under Nikita Khrushchev might move beyond
simply improving the atmosphere in which its relations with
the West were conducted to reassessing its position on such
crucial issues as the German question. This prospect, supported
by evidence of continuing co-operation between the United
States and the Soviet Union in limited areas of common
interest, gave the impression that an East–West *détente* was
developing both on the level of superpower relations and of
intra-European politics.

A significant change occurred when the collective leadership
under Leonid Brezhnev and Alexei Kosygin succeeded Nikita
Khrushchev in October 1964. Their political style was as
cautious as Khrushchev's had been bold. Moreover, the
escalation of hostilities in Vietnam had an unfavourable effect
on East–West relations. Therefore, in spite of some progress
on issues of arms regulation, the feeling that the superpower
détente was progressing simply petered out.[1] That did not stop
progress towards East–West *rapprochement* in Europe, partly
because Soviet policy differentiated between the United States
and its West European allies, and partly because the allies of
both superpowers had more freedom of action. A characteristic feature distinguishing the European *détente* of 1966–8 from
preceding periods of relaxed tension was the fact that poly-
centrism in both camps had reached a far more advanced stage.
Indeed there was an inclination, at least in the West, to take
the continued disintegration of blocs for granted. That, in
addition to the sobering effect of the first superpower confrontation under conditions of rough nuclear parity, and—probably
more important—the vested interest of many West European
politicians in interpreting the European situation in terms of
détente, made the latter appear as almost irreversible.

However, the new Eastern policy initiated by the West
German government of the Grand Coalition in 1967 induced
Moscow to undertake a basic shift in its stand, the full implications of which became clear only with the invasion of Czechoslovakia. The campaign for ' European security ' launched by

[1] Superior figures refer to Notes at p. 129.

the Soviet Union in 1966 primarily with a view to eroding American influence in Western Europe was henceforth formulated in increasingly defensive terms clearly aimed at containing the forces of change in Eastern Europe, which, Moscow seemed to fear, threatened its predominance in the area.[2]

Thus, early 1967 constitutes a watershed in East–West relations in Europe. In the West, the activation of West Germany's Eastern policy even more than the lingering Franco-American controversy about NATO focused attention on some of the basic issues of Western policy and their inter-relation: the future of Western defence arrangements, the prospect for West European unification, and the scope and procedure for accommodation with the Soviet Union and her East European allies. In the East, the cautious differentiation of official stands that emerged in the wake of the campaign for European security and co-operation was thereafter inhibited by the more rigid and defensive Soviet attitudes. Yet, even during the crisis in Czechoslovakia, different nuances in official Eastern statements continued to be visible, presumably reflect-ing divergences in priorities and preferences.

The invasion of Czechoslovakia represents the other main watershed of the period and demonstrated Moscow's urgent preoccupation with consolidating its sphere of influence in Eastern Europe. It also revealed that this concern not only required the unqualified deference of the East European ruling élites to Moscow's wishes on major issues of foreign policy, but ultimately also implied a right of the Soviet Union to control, and if necessary suppress, internal processes of liberal-ization and democratization in Eastern Europe. The invasion showed how much less the Soviet leaders cared about *détente* than about their firm control over Eastern Europe; it also brought into focus the discrepancies that had existed all the time between Western and Soviet conceptions of *détente* in Europe.

The pronouncements of most West European leaders and of some of the less exposed governments in Eastern Europe during the autumn of 1968 seemed to bear witness to their persistent wish to salvage or revive the forces of *détente* and

East–West co-operation in Europe in spite of events in Czecho-slovakia. But the apparent determination of the Soviet leaders to enforce their hegemonic claim in Eastern Europe and the attempt to legalize it through the proclamation of the so-called Brezhnev doctrine of limited sovereignty created great uncertainty about the prospects for a new round of East–West *rapprochement* in Europe. More than ever, such a *rapprochement* seemed to be dependent on developments in the Soviet Union.

Methodology

A study of this kind raises basic questions of methodology, as, for example, the distinction between ' official ' and ' real ' goals, and the extent to which policy declarations, once enunciated, determine the scope for future choices. It is not my intention here to embark upon a long discussion of these and similar methodological issues, but I do wish to make clear my contention about the nature of the conclusions that can be derived from an analysis of foreign policy statements.

I start from the assumption that whatever the ' real ' intentions of policy-makers—which historians may be able to ascertain, at best, decades from now—the actions of party and government bureaucracies are directed towards certain desired outcomes. These goals may be more or less clearly defined by the decision-makers, but their very existence is here postulated as a significant operational factor in the making of foreign policy. Sometimes conflicting views within a policy-making body may inhibit decisions to act in accordance with any given goal. Yet, sooner or later, one among the contending groups and views is likely to prevail; or a compromise may emerge, allowing or requiring a decision that will be in accordance with a specific choice among alternative outcomes or preferences.

I have further assumed here that it is possible to deduce at least the general character of these goals or preferences from a careful analysis of official declarations.

The validity of these assumptions may be questioned on the ground that the predominance of domestic politics in most advanced societies makes it difficult to ascertain whether the formulation of any given official declaration, outwardly dealing with foreign policy issues, has not been determined primarily by domestic considerations. The difficulty is especially great during periods characterized by the absence of an extreme external threat and consequently of any single organizing idea. It can be argued, therefore, that at such times foreign policy statements are no more than *ex post facto* rationalizations.

This objection does not seem to invalidate our previous assumption, however, for although we may never be sure why it was decided to word a given declaration in some particular way, we can reasonably expect that the effects the chosen formulation will have on other governments are taken into consideration in the first place. Therefore, even if the wording of a certain foreign policy declaration is strongly influenced by other considerations, the goals of the country's foreign policy cannot be completely distorted. Indeed the close interrelation between domestic and foreign policy puts a premium on consistency in all public official declarations. This is especially true in modern industrial societies, which have developed a complex socio-technological system for the production and distribution of the goods and services required by their inhabitants. The proper growth and functioning of this vulnerable system presupposes that guide-lines are issued which meet certain minimum requirements of reliability and accessibility. Foreign policy expectations reflected in official declarations constitute an important parameter for the formulation of such guide-lines. The relationship between the evolution of strategic doctrine and the procurement of weapons for the armed forces in the United States is perhaps the most obvious case in point. Statements by American officials on strategic matters are usually rightly treated as declarations of intent bearing both on a vital sector of the American economy and on United States foreign relations. These statements can in some cases be regarded as signals to the Soviet Union,[3] and their reliability as such is enhanced by the fact that they constitute at the same time guide-lines for the allocation of national resources.

I have examined foreign policy declarations primarily as a source reflecting the goals and preferences of decision-makers. Another aspect, which I have only touched on here and there, is the effect which declarations have as limits on the formation of future policy. It is difficult to demonstrate this effect, or to assess its weight in particular situations. Indeed, it could be argued that governments and officials in most countries have developed an appreciable capacity for presenting novel initiatives as being compatible with earlier positions. Yet the pressures for genuine consistency are strong in most bureaucracies, and the formal limits set by earlier declarations can therefore seldom be completely disregarded.

For this study I have examined a great number of official and semi-official pronouncements, only a fraction of which are accounted for in the text and footnotes. The criterion for including any one document has been my judgement as to whether it represented an official position and reflected a significant nuance in the over-all spectrum of a given government's general posture. No attempt has been made to apply any rigid structure in selecting relevant material, but the focus for all countries analysed has been on the nature, implications, and potentialities of East–West relations in Europe during 1966–8.

I have divided foreign policy into 'declaratory policy' and 'action policy' to make a distinction between what a government says about various issues and what it actually does to influence conditions in the international environment to its advantage. Although I have been concerned mainly with the analysis of declaratory policy, I have not been able to disregard action policy altogether, for two reasons. Firstly, an absolutely clear distinction between the two is not feasible: declarations can sometimes be legitimately considered as actions. Secondly, some of the moves of the main actors in the East–West drama have had to be mentioned briefly in order to provide the proper background for an understanding of the declaratory stands adopted by different governments.

At times it has also been difficult to distinguish between short-term and long-term policy proposals. In general, immediate policy requirements are linked up with official views of the prevailing European situation, while long-term policy proposals have been conceived as steps on the road to a European settlement. On the other hand, it is obvious that long-term programmes such as those contained in the policy declaration made in December 1966 by the new government in West Germany or the Karlovy Vary statement issued by the Conference of Communist and Workers' Parties in April 1967 should also be seen as the result of an assessment of immediate policy requirements. Ultimately, the analysis of both serves to identify the priorities of a given government or élite group.

The purpose of this study could thus be defined as being to offer an interpretation of the preferences and goals of the major actors on the European scene based on their declaratory policy during the period 1966–8, and to identify against this background certain requirements for a more stable *modus vivendi* and possible reconciliation in Europe.

I should like to conclude this introduction on a personal note. I was born a German citizen, spent most of my childhood in Poland and my adolescence in Sweden. These early experiences have given me a special interest in the subject-matter of the present book, and perhaps also some special insight. Although I have attempted to keep this study balanced, my Western background and my political orientation have necessarily influenced both the analysis and the conclusions. I should like to think that even those who cannot accept the latter will be inclined to recognize that I have made a sincere effort to see the problems from the point of view of all the main parties involved.

THE WEST AND THE EUROPEAN DÉTENTE, 1966–1968

THIS chapter is devoted to an examination of how the decision-makers in each of the main Western states* officially described the nature of East–West relations and what policy conclusions, short-term as well as long-term, they drew from their perceptions. One should bear in mind when assessing the significance of official descriptions of the international situation at any given moment, that they are imperfect reflections of the true perceptions of decision-makers. Furthermore the perceptions themselves are always influenced to some extent by the preferred policy choices of the government in question. A government may see more or less of a rising or declining threat, of an emerging or disappearing opportunity, according to whether—for some reason which may be external to the issue—such a perception suits its purposes. Admittedly, there are limits to this kind of manipulation of official Western views: with regard to East–West relations in Europe they would seem to be posed by the stark evidence of a potential Soviet threat on the one hand, and by some tangible inhibitions to Soviet expansionism on the other. But it can be demonstrated that the leeway for different interpretations of the nature, requirements, and potentialities of the European situation was nevertheless significant.

These differences in interpretation were largely due to the fact that, as the common concern for the security of Western Europe abated, forces of national self-assertion were released within each of the member-countries of the Western alliance. The reality of a certain amount of *détente* in Europe, and the

*The states considered here are the US, the UK, France, and West Germany. Though Italy was active in developing bilateral ties with the USSR and East European countries—a policy that was given a wider basis when the Fanfani plan for technological co-operation between East and West was put forward in Oct. 1966—she did not bear the same responsibilities as the other main Western countries and therefore tended to leave the initiative to them.

notion that a new, more satisfactory relationship with the East could and should be promoted by efforts on the part of the West, provided a respectable opportunity for individual Western states to take up policy postures which were more directly adapted to their major national aspirations and pre-occupations. Thus it became more apparent that the import-ance which the main Western governments attributed to East–West relations in Europe differed significantly. In addition, the greater fluidity of the European situation brought into the open their different preferences with regard to the shape of a conceivable Europe-wide configuration, and of its relations with the superpowers. In view of the divergences in outlook and priorities and the absence of any overriding common concern, it is not surprising that the period of *détente* in Europe during 1966–8 confronted the West with formidable problems of policy co-ordination.

France

France was the first of the West European countries to take advantage of the greater freedom of movement available to America's allies as a result of the relaxation of tension between the superpowers. President de Gaulle's veto of the British application for membership of the EEC in January 1963 demonstrated his determination to prevent what he considered an Anglo-Saxon plot to maintain American hegemony over Western Europe and his resoluteness to assert French and European independence. A number of general circumstances enabled France to adopt this independent line of policy. Despite de Gaulle's questioning the credibility of the American deterrent, France, like the rest of Western Europe, was pro-tected by the nuclear umbrella of the United States. Unlike West Germany, however, France was geographically one step removed from the central area of confrontation and could therefore show correspondingly less concern about the threat of more ambiguous Soviet challenges. At the same time, the increase in domestic stability resulting from the end of the Algerian war and the propitious effects of the reforms of the Fifth Republic released economic and political resources. The crucial factor, however, was undoubtedly de Gaulle himself, for he had the political will to mobilize and use those resources in support of his vision of a future Europe.

The Gaullist concept of a stable peace in Europe had as its central feature the re-emergence of a Europe independent 'from one end to the other of the territory which nature has given it'.* This meant a Europe embracing all states on the continent, including the Soviet Union (or 'Russia', as the General preferred to say), a Europe working in harmony and co-operation to develop her vast resources and eventually fulfil a world role commensurate with her human and economic potential. The reappearance of a European order of this kind would both permit and require a solution to the German problem. France's approach to the settlement of this question —' *the* European problem ', as de Gaulle termed it at his press conference on 4 February 1965—was formulated by him as an effort ' to see that Germany henceforth becomes a definite element of progress and peace; on this condition to help with its reunification; to make a start and select the framework which would make this possible '.[1]

To de Gaulle such a framework was as exclusively European as possible. For example, at the same press conference he called upon the European peoples to ' envisage first examining together, then settling in common, and lastly guaranteeing conjointly the solution to the question which is essentially that of their continent '.[2] The contention sometimes inferred from these and similar statements that de Gaulle wished to exclude the United States from a *settlement* in Central Europe appears hardly warranted, however. Quite apart from the fact that it implies a gross underestimation of his political realism, a number of official French pronouncements pointed in a different direction.[3] The General's position was that the essential preconditions for the solution of the German question should be created by the European countries themselves through a process of *rapprochement* and increased bilateral co-operation.

---

*This presentation is limited to de Gaulle's views not only because he largely determined French foreign policy during the period studied, but also because there is a distinct continuity in the conduct of French foreign relations. Therefore, the central elements in the Gaullist grand design for Europe may very well outlive its creator.

The ultimate settlement, however, would have to be endorsed by the United States as well.[4]

This is not to deny that a fundamental feature of the Gaullist grand design for a future Europe was to dismantle the super-power hegemonies and thus to bring about an eventual American withdrawal from Western Europe both in terms of military presence and political leadership. Yet, this process of European ' liberation ' was to take place under the protective nuclear umbrella of the United States, which would be disposed of only when a new ' equilibrium ' in Europe had enabled Europe to settle its own problems. The General explained how that was to be brought about at his thirteenth press conference on 21 February 1966:

The Union of the Six [members of the EEC], once achieved, and all the more if it comes to be supplemented then by new European memberships and associations, can and must be, towards the United States, a valid partner in all areas, I mean powerful and independent. The Union of the Six can and must also be one of the piers on which will gradually be built first the equilibrium, then the cooperation and then, perhaps one day, the union of all Europe which would enable our Continent to settle its own problems peacefully, particularly, that of Germany, including its reunification.[5]

A unified Western Europe was thus conceived by de Gaulle not only as an independent partner of the United States but also as an integral element of a pan-European system in which by its own weight it could constitute a force countervailing the power of the Soviet Union.[6] The two main pillars of this system were presumably to be Paris and Moscow, which presupposed a significant rise in rank for France.

As for Eastern Europe, the Gaullist vision assumed that ' Russia ' would evolve ' in such a way that it sees its future not through totalitarian restraint imposed on its land and on others, but through progress accomplished in common by free men and peoples '. This would also imply that the nations which had been ' satellized ' by Moscow would ' be able to play their role in a renewed Europe '.

The modalities of a German settlement, included in de Gaulle's long-range programme, implied that a united

Germany (and by implication the Federal Republic) would have to accept limitations on its armaments (presumably qualitative as well as quantitative) and that it would have to recognize the borders drawn up at Potsdam as definite.[7]

A fundamental premise of General de Gaulle's vision for a future Europe was that the individuality of European nations and states be reasserted. For him the nation-state was the only philosophically justifiable unit to which an individual could give his loyalty in return for the security to live freely. The General followed this principle with a consistency often maddening to his allies and embarrassing to his countrymen —for example, when it came to relations with Canada. In his design for Europe, it led him to oppose any devolution of national sovereignty to supranational organs. The building of Europe must be done through the co-operative efforts of sovereign governments acting according to their own interests. Ultimately he saw a greater potential for a lasting community of interests among these revitalized nations of the European continent, including the Russians, than among those around the North Atlantic.

Détente in Europe was a necessary precondition for the realization of the General's grand scheme. For that reason, he was more inclined than any other Western leader to perceive an improvement in East–West relations as a genuine relaxation of tension. Thus, on 29 July 1963, shortly after the American-British-Soviet agreement to sign a partial test ban treaty had been announced, he held a press conference at which he argued that one should entertain the possibility that Moscow was pursuing a sincere policy of peaceful coexistence. He identified the following as the main forces that tended to push the USSR in that direction: (a) the ' human evolution ' in the Soviet Union and its satellite states; (b) the economic and social difficulties in those countries; and (c) the emerging Sino–Soviet conflict. France, he asserted, had believed for a long time that the day might come when a real *détente* and even a sincere *entente* would permit a complete change in East–West relations; she would then make some constructive propositions with regard to Europe's peace, equilibrium, and destiny.[8]

By 1966 President de Gaulle and his ministers were describing

the European situation in terms indicating that they believed
that the possibilities foreseen by the French President three
years earlier were rapidly materializing.   On 3 November
1966 the French foreign minister, Couve de Murville, told the
National Assembly that for some time, and particularly during
1966, France's relations with the socialist countries of Eastern
Europe had been changing radically.   ' From formal, infre-
quent and negative ', he asserted, ' they have become numerous,
cordial, constructive, and all told, normal.'[9]   And de Gaulle
himself asserted in his New Year message on 31 December
1966 that the cold war was ' in the process of disappearing '.
France, who had regained her independence, would, he
assured his audience, ' continue to direct her action toward
continental *rapprochement* '.[10]

Thus, at least from 1966 on, the French government attempted to promote the notion of a progressively developing
European *détente*.   To provide a slogan describing East–West
relations in Europe in dynamic terms, de Gaulle began to
speak of *détente* leading to *entente* and eventually to *coopération*
embracing all Europe.[11]   He acknowledged the importance of
the nuclear stalemate between the superpowers for the preservation of peace, but he always emphasized the precarious and
basically static nature of that relationship, which, in his view,
could not produce reconciliation in Europe.   For that to
occur, he argued, it would be necessary to overcome the confrontation and restore Europe's unity; this undertaking the
General consistently presented as a task for Europeans ' from
the Atlantic to the Urals '.[12]   By describing the improvement
of East–West relations in Europe as a dynamic and self-
contained process, de Gaulle all but ignored the—admittedly
limited—relaxation of tension between the superpowers as an
essential precondition for European *détente*.   He took this
factor into account in a negative way only, as a potential
external threat to an otherwise steadily progressing amelioration of relations in Europe.[13]

The most important French policy measures related to the
emergence of *détente* in Europe were to withdraw from NATO's
military organization, and to multiply its bilateral contacts
with the Soviet Union and Eastern Europe.   The first move

was made in the grandest Gaullist fashion, on the eve of the
General's visit to Moscow in 1966, to underline the point
that it was a step in the direction of the ' European Europe '
he so strongly advocated as the appropriate context for a
lasting peaceful order in Europe. The French government
depicted the increase in its bilateral relations with Eastern
Europe as a major contribution to European reconciliation
and security.[14] While the primary aim of this policy was to
present France as a worthy partner to Russia in Europe, it
was also meant to encourage a pan-European orientation
among the smaller East European states, which by necessity
would imply a lessening of those countries' dependence on
Moscow. The underlying incompatibility of these two lines
of policy remained dormant, however.[15]

To sum up, it appears that the French government in its
official declarations ascribed the inception of the European
détente process to a basic and permanent change in Soviet
foreign policy. The emerging opportunities for a radical
alteration in East–West relations in Europe induced France to
reactivate old, and open up new, channels of contact and
communication between the two parts of Europe, thus increasing the momentum of the trend towards a European
reconciliation. This development was considered in Paris to
be virtually irreversible if Europe were not disturbed by
' external ' influence,[16] and eventually it would both permit
and require the transformation of the alliance systems.

The United Kingdom

During the late 1950s Britain was confronted with the
necessity to recast its relations with Europe. Consecutive
British governments had tried to postpone making a clear
choice between maintaining Britain's world-wide commitments
and concentrating its efforts on developing its position in
Europe. Britain's special ties with the United States figured
prominently in these calculations. One reason for British
reluctance to throw in its lot with the Europeans was concern
that, by becoming one of several roughly equal West European
countries, it would lose its special leverage in Washington.
When against British expectations West European integration

made great strides forward, London was faced with the prospect of being overshadowed in Washington by a formidable West European combination, and at the same time having no influence within that combination. A wait-and-see policy was thus no longer possible, and in 1961 the Macmillan government made the historic decision to seek membership of the EEC.[17]

Even then, however, Britain's outlook continued to bear the imprint of the traditions of global commitments. Throughout the 1960s those British politicians favouring their country's entry into the Common Market claimed that Britain's contribution to a unified Western Europe would be to make it more outward-looking and able to shoulder wider responsibilities. They pursued this line of thought to argue that British membership of a West European combination would facilitate East–West reconciliation in Europe.[18]

The British government lacked a clear official ' vision ' of a possible settlement in Europe. One reason for that was certainly Britain's traditional pragmatic approach to policy, her reluctance to take a stand on hypothetical issues or on subjects that have not become ' mature '. However, another consideration was probably more important, especially in the latter half of the 1960s. Since there were differences of view between Paris and Bonn with regard to the ultimate shape of a European settlement,[19] Britain would risk further complicating her efforts to join the EEC if she clarified her own stand on the Central European issues and adopted a position that would be likely to displease one or both of her main continental partners.[20] A third and underlying influence was that the British public and politicians—particularly those in the Labour party —had mixed feelings about all things German. This also disinclined the government from publicly discussing problems so inextricably bound up with Germany's future. Consequently, apart from occasional remarks to the effect that the rift across Europe ought to be healed peacefully and Germany reconstituted—although not beyond the Oder–Neisse line [21]— the official British attitude was marked by an almost complete absence of references to the particulars of a European settlement.

The British government was less reticent about the means which in its view would be conducive to the long-term goal of East–West reconciliation. Like most other Western governments, it recommended increasing contacts and co-operation between European countries across the dividing line, bilaterally as well as multilaterally. In the late 1950s and early 1960s the Macmillan government took a number of initiatives—including summit talks with the Russians—in order to explore the scope for East–West agreements on disarmament questions and other major international issues. On the whole, the Labour government, which came into power in late 1964, was interested in promoting arms control measures in Europe but its diplomacy in this field was less grandiose than its predecessor's, primarily, it would seem, to avoid giving offence to Britain's potential EEC partners. Earlier and with greater emphasis than other Western states, Britain advocated measures that would reduce the scale and risks of the military confrontation in Central Europe. These steps, it was usually argued, would foster greater trust between East and West. And on this basis, a state of improved political relations in Europe would emerge, in which it would be possible not only to establish more far-reaching arms control measures in Central Europe, but also to tackle simultaneously the unresolved political issues, including the German question.[22]

On 28 February 1967 Britain's foreign secretary, George Brown, spoke in the House of Commons of the European *détente* as a process ' which is already happening in its early beginnings ' and which he hoped would make mutual reduction of forces to lower levels in Central Europe ' a practical possibility '. Even though this statement was a comparatively cautious one, Mr Brown nevertheless conveyed the impression that he considered East–West relations in Europe to be on the move towards a further easing of tensions and towards greater general stability.[23] His cabinet colleague Denis Healey, Secretary of State for Defence, was even more articulate and optimistic the day before when he presented his views on that same subject to the Commons. He spoke of a prevailing ' political *détente* ', which in his view was ' recognized by every government on both sides of the dividing line ', and alluded to the decision of the NATO Council in December 1966 to use every possible means of extending it. Mr Healey then proceeded to analyse its foundations. He saw 'solid reasons' for a basic change in Soviet attitudes towards the West, the main ones being the strengthening of Western Europe (primarily through NATO), the profound political and economic transformation of Soviet society, the emergence of China as a formidable yet only potential threat to the Soviet Union, and, last but not least, the risk of nuclear escalation confronting any potential aggressor in Central Europe. In his opinion it was difficult to imagine that Soviet policy, being rooted in these hard facts, could change overnight so fundamentally that Moscow could contemplate a war in Europe.[24]

Largely the same estimation of the threat from the Soviet Union appeared in the government's White Paper on defence for 1967, although the wording there was more cautious. The policy implications that the government drew from these assessments were summarized in the following terms:

The British Government believes that both the political and military extension of the *détente* would best be achieved by mutual reduction of the forces of the NATO and Warsaw Pact powers. This measure of arms control, besides giving both sides greater security, would create a better climate in which to approach the major political problems of the European continent, and would liberate resources for the economy.[25]

It is worth noting that the specific policy proposal of mutual force reductions put forward by the British government was embedded in a wider conception of promoting arms control agreements in Central Europe as a preliminary but essential step towards improving East–West relations. The Labour government had earlier supported other arms control measures for Central Europe—such as establishing observation posts on both sides of the dividing line—with similar arguments. It had argued that, although political evolution and arms control should in principle go hand in hand, a start must be made somewhere, and in the prevailing European situation, that could best be done in the field of arms control.[26] The force reduction proposals were conceived in the same way. When later economic constraints induced the British to consider scaling down the Rhine Army in spite of the absence of any indications that the USSR might follow suit, the primary economic motivation for the proposed steps was revealed.

It seems clear then that the British government was anxious to present one of its major national problems, the need for a sustained economic recovery, in terms compatible with the international requirements of *détente* in Europe. Indeed, it is indicative of the importance attributed by Whitehall to maintaining this compatibility that the government went to considerable lengths to justify British membership of the EEC, the other major concern of Britain's leaders at that time, as a contribution to improving East–West relations in Europe.[27] That position was characteristic not only of the governing Labour party, but also of the Conservative Opposition.[28] On balance, the British seemed confident that the European *détente* would last and they were therefore anxious to use it in order to cut defence expenditure, to make the military environment more secure, and thus to create the climatic preconditions for an eventual political settlement.

The United States of America

The main goals of American foreign policy towards Europe have remained basically unaltered throughout the post-war period. They have focused on the creation of a viable Western Europe as a partner to the United States. In the late 1940s that appeared to be a formidable task because the West European states were economically weak and politically unstable, and because the Soviet Union appeared to pose an overwhelming threat to their security. Ten years later the situation had changed fundamentally. Economic recuperation had been largely achieved, thanks mainly to the massive American aid under the Marshall Plan. In addition, six of the countries had embarked on a process of economic integration which seemed to open up prospects for far-reaching political unification in Western Europe. At the same time, the security of Western Europe had been ensured by the creation of NATO, which provided a framework for joint Western defence and a guarantee of American involvement on the European continent.

The very success of these measures generated new problems

for the alliance. A sense of self-confidence emerged in Western
Europe as a result of which policy co-ordination within the
alliance became increasingly difficult. These centripetal
tendencies coincided with a stage in the development of nuclear
strategy at which central control appeared to American policy-
makers absolutely essential. Consequently, there arose an
American predilection for devising schemes that would some-
how channel these new economic and political pressures into
a direction consistent with American economic interests and
with the demand that ultimate decisions about peace and war
should rest with Washington. President Kennedy's Grand
Design to create in Western Europe a partner of equal political
weight and responsibility within the alliance faltered—only
partly because of French resistance. It seemed after the
Cuban crisis that President Kennedy was determined to
improve relations with Russia and did not want the special
preferences of the West European allies to stand in the way
of his efforts to bring about a global *détente*. In addition,
Washington's propensity to promote its own model for the
organization of Western Europe was resented by some allied
governments. This reaction was even more apparent in the
case of the other American scheme, the plan for a multilateral
nuclear force, and it also came to nothing. By the mid-1960s
these setbacks had created a natural disinclination in Washington to take new initiatives in its European policy, an attitude
reinforced by the shift in attention to the conflict in Vietnam
that occurred in 1965.

In the meantime, the European *détente*, which had developed
out of the relaxation of tension between the superpowers after
the Cuban crisis, continued to progress. By the spring of 1966
this development had reached a stage at which General de
Gaulle deemed the time ripe to leave the integrated command
structure of NATO. This event dramatized the simmering
crisis within the Western alliance, and speeded up the reassessment of American policy towards Europe which had run into
the doldrums.

Official descriptions of the European détente
   Official American descriptions of the more amiable East–West

relations in Europe of the mid-1960s were clearly tinged
by the crisis in the alliance.   In July 1966, Mr Harlan Cleveland, American permanent representative on the NATO
Council, defined *détente* as ' a state of relations in which tensions
have been relaxed to safe levels ' and argued for ' a systematic
search . . . for a greater degree of *détente*, for an atmosphere in
which fundamental issues might be resolved '.[29]   He thus
seemed to imply that some limited degree of *détente* had been
reached but that tensions had not yet been reduced to ' safe
levels '.   What Mr Cleveland chose to call ' real *détente* '
would be reached only after the Soviet Union had concluded
that it was in its interest ' to come to a peaceful and reasonable
settlement of the fundamental issues in Europe '.[30]

Similarly, in April 1967, Under Secretary of State Nicholas
de B. Katzenbach distinguished between a *détente* that was
simply an easing of American–Soviet tensions—the existence
of which he acknowledged—and ' a large-scale *détente* ' that
was tantamount to an *elimination* of the basic issues of the cold
war, which in his view would be achieved only with the
emergence of ' a stable and secure Europe '.[31]

Thus the American government seemed anxious to warn its
allies that the prevailing situation in Europe was nothing more
than a limited improvement in relations which did not meet
the basic requirements for a settlement of the outstanding
issues.   Spelling out the preconditions for this distinctly limited
détente, Eugene V. Rostow, Under Secretary of State for
Political Affairs, stressed that it required ' a mutual respect
for the principle that there be no unilateral changes of the
frontiers of the systems by force, or by the threat of force '.[32]
The emphasis on this ' prudent rule of reciprocal safety ', as
Mr Rostow called it, also reflected an American inclination to
differentiate between a situation in which conflicts could be
kept under control and a situation conducive to the settlement
of basic disputes.   In addition, the pronouncements of American officials were focused on the security aspect of relations
with the Soviet Union, thereby suggesting that the degree of
détente that had been achieved was primarily the result of
Western solidarity.   These perceptions clearly distinguished
the American position from that of General de Gaulle, who,

as we have seen, described the European *détente* mainly in terms of the multiplication of bilateral relations between European states and as a process which was well under way and naturally evolving towards reconciliation.[33]

Effects of the European détente on US foreign policy

If by 1965 there was a certain void in American policy initiatives towards Europe it was not for lack of ideas among American policy-makers and their consultants. Old concepts which had taken root in the State Department many years earlier, such as Atlantic Partnership, continued to have a significant impact on the conduct of American foreign policy. At the same time new priorities and ideas were introduced into the official debate by the Department of Defense—more influential under its assertive secretary, Robert McNamara, than it had ever been, the Arms Control and Disarmament Agency (ACDA), newly formed in 1962, and numerous analysts and observers inside and outside the government. These new suggestions were largely centred on the problems of arms control and nuclear proliferation which had gained urgency after the Chinese demonstrated their nuclear capability in October 1964. William C. Foster, director of ACDA, brought the conflict of priorities between different factions within the administration into focus when he argued that some ' erosion of alliances resulting from the high degree of US–Soviet cooperation . . . will be required if a non-proliferation programme is to be successful '.[34] This reasoning met with reservations from those in the State Department who considered that the cohesion of NATO ought to have the highest priority. The Atlanticist orientation favoured by these officials was challenged from several quarters, however, not only from those concerned about the primacy of American–Soviet relations, but also from others who advocated new formulas for transatlantic configurations.

George W. Ball, the second most senior official in the Department of State, represented the traditional position in the Department during this whole period when in the summer of 1966 he argued in favour of concentrating on the promotion of West European unification and the adaptation of NATO to the requirements of 'equal partnership' not only as a goal in itself but also as the proper road towards a European settlement. In his view, only Western unity achieved in this way would be likely to induce the Soviet government to change its policy, a change which he considered the essential precondition for European and German reunification.[35] An alternative approach was recommended by Zbigniew Brzezinski who was a member of the Policy Planning Council of the State Department during part of this period. In his testimony to the House of Representatives Subcommittee on Foreign Affairs on 28 April 1966 he held the view that NATO could be saved only if a wider initiative to bring about reconciliation between East and West in Europe were undertaken, and suggested therefore that the United States should propose a conference of the heads of Western governments in order to elaborate common proposals for the development of multilateral ties with the Soviet Union and Eastern Europe as a first step.[36] Finally, on 27 April 1966 during the same period of reappraisal of American policy towards Europe, Henry Kissinger argued that ' the diplomacy for the unification of Europe has to be different from the strategy for the defense of Europe '. He therefore advised in favour of creating a European structure specially devised to conduct negotiations with the East. This structure would be protected by the United States but would constitute an entity distinct from the Western defence alliance.[37]

In view of these and other differences of opinion among American policy-makers and their advisers, it is not surprising that the highest officials of the United States limited themselves in their statements to emphasizing the conventional wisdom: that cohesion and solidarity among the Western states was a necessary precondition for a European settlement.[38]

While the government of the United States emphatically committed itself to the ultimate goal of a European settlement and to the reunification of Germany, it refrained from presenting long-term proposals that could be called a programme for peace in Europe. Nevertheless, as a consequence of the change in the East–West climate American policy on relations with Eastern Europe and on the German question had become ripe for reassessment, and the modifications that took place showed traces of the ideas discussed above.

Ever since the upheavals of 1956 in Eastern Europe the United States had sought to promote an evolutionary process of change in the direction of greater national self-assertion in Eastern Europe by a cautious and selectively applied policy of expanding trade and cultural contacts with individual countries of the region. This policy became official doctrine under President Kennedy, but its implementation was for many years hampered by the high level of East–West tension. It did not have much practical significance therefore until the relaxation that followed the Cuban missile crisis.[39]

In May 1964 President Johnson used the *bridge-building* metaphor for the first time to describe active efforts to implement the policy.[40] The aim of these efforts remained largely unchanged during the following years. As Under Secretary of State Averell Harriman put it, this aspect of American foreign policy was designed to encourage ' a progressive loosening of external authority over Eastern European countries and the continuing reassertion of national autonomy and diversity '.[41] The policy may not have been designed to instigate hostility between Russia and her allies, but it was clearly intended to act as a force that would erode Soviet and communist influence in the East European countries.[42] It could therefore be argued—and the USSR did not fail to do so—that the policy of ' peaceful engagement ' was really only a more sophisticated form of the old rollback strategy aiming at the same end result: ' liberation '.

By 1966, however, there had emerged a new element in this policy, which put it in a different perspective. The State Department had apparently come to the conclusion that in order to retain credibility and some leverage in Eastern Europe the United States must explicitly disavow any intention of subverting communist governments in Eastern Europe or exploiting differences between Moscow and her East European allies.[43] This did not mean that the US government had abandoned its hopes of increasing the autonomy of the communist states in Eastern Europe. But it *did* make a difference whether the attainment of that result was explicitly presented as a main motivation for American foreign policy, or if it seemed to be tacitly assumed as a likely consequence. The chief motivation for ' peaceful engagement ' now appeared to be Washington's desire to promote a comprehensive East–West reconciliation in Europe. This new interpretation of American policy towards the Soviet Union and Eastern Europe was given the highest sanction in President Johnson's major speech of 7 October 1966 on the unfinished task of ' making Europe whole '.[44]

One of the main proponents of ' peaceful engagement ', Mr Zbigniew Brzezinski, expounded its basic *raison d'être* in a speech in Ottawa in early 1967. He emphasized that the United States did not intend to seek an immediate settlement, particularly not over the heads of the Europeans. The purpose of the policy was to engage all, including both the Soviet Union and Eastern Europe, in a process of gradual change. Brzezinski added:

I am convinced it would be idle, and probably counterproductive, to concentrate on stimulating East European nationalism or hostility to the Soviet Union; to be sure, the more independence there is in the East, the better—but as a means and not as an end in itself. Some East European countries can act as transmission belts by moving ahead of the Soviet Union, but not for the purpose of separating themselves entirely from the Soviet Union—rather for the purpose of promoting a different kind of East–West relationship.[45]

In this statement Brzezinski made no reference to how East Germany fitted into the policy of ' peaceful engagement '. This omission may have been an indication of a change in American thinking on that theme, for Brzezinski had earlier been a forceful advocate of isolating East Germany from the other East European states.[46] By 1967 the official American attitude towards East Germany seemed to have evolved from non-recognition and active isolation to a position which is probably best described by the word ' silence '.*

*Some European observers interpret this silence as tantamount to *de facto* recognition of the GDR. The most significant feature of US policy towards East Germany in 1967 was, however, the apparent inclination of the administration to follow West Germany's lead—once Bonn had decided to include intra-German relations in its *détente* policy.

A second result of the attempts of the United States to revise its European policy was that it clarified its stand on the German question. It took some time, however, before the American position on the German problem could be fully harmonized with her East European policy to make a coherent whole. This may have been partly due to feelings in West Germany, where the process of adjusting to the new realities of the Central European situation was more difficult and more time-consuming than elsewhere in the West.

Having earlier argued against any steps toward *détente* without some progress in the direction of reunification—lest the division of Germany be viewed as permanent—the Bonn government now had difficulty in accepting the position that *détente* in Europe was a necessary *precondition* for reunification. The American government avoided complete clarity on this issue. In May 1964 President Johnson emphasized the belief of the American government that ' wise and skilful development of relationships with the nations of Eastern Europe can speed the day when Germany will be reunited '.[47] According to Mr Brzezinski, this speech ' marked the final abandonment of the notion that the German problem could be settled outside of, or prior to, an overall change in relations of the two halves of Europe '.[48] It did not indicate official support for the view already prevalent in Washington at that time that *détente* in Europe was both possible and desirable without any simultaneous steps in the direction of German reunification. A clearer linkage between European *détente* and German reunification was presented by President Johnson on 7 October 1966, when he said: ' In a restored Europe, Germany can and will be united. This remains a vital purpose of American policy. It can only be accomplished through a growing reconciliation. There is no short-cut.' [49] This was the first time that the main spokesman of the leading Western power explicitly stated that German reunification could be attained only by way of a progressive *détente*, by shaping a ' new political environment ' in Europe. His statement implied that German reunification could come only at the end of a long process of reconciliation.

In an even broader sense the President's speech of 7 October

1966 represented an attempt to make American policy in Europe more coherent, for it emphasized the fundamental interdependence between Western unity and the East–West *détente* in Europe. This portion of the address clearly reflected a compromise between the ' Atlanticists ' and the ' bridge-builders ' in the Johnson administration. The President raised the fundamental issues without indicating any distinct preference for any particular future line of action. He said that ' one great goal of a united West [would be] to heal the wound in Europe which now cuts East from West and brother from brother ', and it was with this great task in mind that he advocated the ' vigorous pursuit of further unity in the West '. [50] The President also spoke of ' a united Western Europe ' that could ' move more confidently in peaceful initiatives toward the East ', but he did not clarify *how* a closer relation between the United States and a more unified Western Europe could promote East–West reconciliation.[51]

An unalterable element in the official American position regarding a European settlement was nevertheless the permanent character of America's involvement in European affairs and more specifically in the defence of Western Europe.[52] The institutional framework for this involvement was not detailed, but a predilection for retaining the present alliance system for the foreseeable future—although possibly with some modifications that would take into account the greater independence of the West European states—was a conspicuous feature in most official declarations from Washington.[53]

The hopes and fears for an active American involvement in the process of East–West reconciliation which the October 1966 speech raised in Europe were soon dampened. The legislative measures proposed by the US administration in support of its policy of building bridges to the East encountered strong opposition in Congress. Congressmen had shown little inclination to adopt the State Department's position of differentiating between communist governments,[54] and the escalation of the war in Vietnam created an atmosphere that made them even less susceptible to such arguments.[55] Since the administration itself was increasingly preoccupied with the Vietnamese conflict and its repercussions, it was not in a position to follow up the new signals hoisted in October 1966.

President Johnson's speech clearly signified that American policy-makers had become aware of the need to recast their basic conceptions with regard to transatlantic relations in order to keep them relevant to the changed East–West constellation in Europe.[56] During the remainder of Johnson's term of office, however, the declarations of American officials on European policy referred back to this speech without breaking new ground.

West Germany

When we turn to West Germany, we deal with a country whose foreign policy was more immediately affected by the legacies of the past. Germany had become the main focus of East–West tension and its future constituted the cardinal problem to be overcome in any attempt to bring an end to the division of Europe. As a result, the provisional state of West Germany was confronted with the difficult task of defining its identity and purpose, safeguarding its security, and yet finding some way to progress towards the ultimate reunification of the German nation.

Konrad Adenauer sought to solve these dilemmas by concentrating on the integration of West Germany in the Western family of nations. This policy achieved for West Germany protection against the Soviet Union and acceptance as an equal member of the Western alliance. In addition, Adenauer argued that it was also the most realistic approach to the problem of German reunification, which could be resolved only from a Western position of strength. According to this view, the West was not to embark on any measures of *détente* towards the East unless they were coupled with steps towards German reunification.[57] A corollary of this attitude was the non-recognition of the GDR, established in 1949, and the policy of considering the recognition of East Germany by third parties as an unfriendly act. This stand was sharpened when Bonn decided to exchange ambassadors with Moscow in 1955. A declaration by the head of the political department of the West German Foreign Office, Professor Wilhelm Grewe, implied that the Federal Republic would have no diplomatic relations with any country recognizing East Germany.[58] This was the origin of the so-called Hallstein doctrine, which for a number of years left a virtual void in West German policy towards Eastern Europe.

In 1961 when the Berlin Wall was erected in the Eastern sector of the city the logic of this policy, which had its opponents even earlier, came under severe attack. A lively domestic debate about the need for a more active Eastern policy led in time to a modification introduced in 1963–4 by Gerhard Schröder who was then the foreign minister. Although there was no change in the goals of West German foreign policy, a new strategy was adopted whereby official contacts below the diplomatic level were established with a number of East European countries. East Germany was excluded from these measures, the purpose being to isolate its regime. There were several indications during this period that policy-makers in Bonn realized that a stable peace required some German sacrifices—for example on the border problems [59]—yet no peace programme was put forward, for it was argued that by doing so the Federal Republic would be giving away essential bargaining assets.

Official West German views of the European situation during the years 1964–6 did not follow the line of change general in the West.[60] This discrepancy was partly due to the fact that the Federal Republic was militarily and politically the most exposed of all the Western allies and felt the pressure on West Berlin more intensely. To the extent, therefore, that the Bonn government acknowledged the existence of Soviet declarations of peaceful intentions at all, it was inclined to see them mainly as the result of Western determination to oppose threats and pressure, or else as some purely tactical device to split the Atlantic alliance and isolate West Germany.[61] This more sceptical attitude should be seen in the light of the special nature of West German threat perceptions. In assessing the magnitude of the danger from the Soviet Union, the other Western powers were mainly concerned with the possibility that Moscow might attempt to alter the *status quo* in Central Europe to its advantage. There was an additional dimension to West German perceptions: the likelihood that the Soviet Union would succeed in permanently denying the German nation its right to self-determination.⁶² Only a reduction of threats against the *status quo* in Europe that did not at the same time aggravate this basic German concern was likely to bring about a significant over-all decrease in their threat perceptions. Consequently, there was a tendency in Bonn to disregard all signs of a change in Soviet attitudes towards the West as long as no evidence was forthcoming that Moscow might be willing to reconsider its fundamental stand on the German problem.

However, a different line of thinking began to assert itself in the West German debate during 1965–6, and it was clearly articulated, for example, by Helmut Schmidt, spokesman on defence matters for the Social Democrats, at the party conference in June 1966. Schmidt described *détente* as a more symmetrical process than had been customary in Bonn. He also defined the foreign policy of the Soviet Union as basically defensive, the purpose of which was to consolidate the Soviet sphere of influence. In his view, the main factors that had produced this limitation in Soviet foreign policy objectives were the nuclear stalemate and domestic pressure sensed by the Soviet leadership for a greater share of national resources to be allocated to the development of Soviet society.⁶³

These ideas were much closer to the mainstream of official Western policy toward the East as it had evolved during 1963–6. Bonn's spontaneously negative reaction to President Johnson's speech of 7 October 1966 ⁶⁴ therefore underlined the fact that an adaptation of the Federal Republic's stand had become absolutely necessary if its isolation within the Western alliance were to be prevented and the way cleared for the evolution of a Western posture towards the East that would satisfy the minimum requirements of consistency and credibility.

By the autumn of 1966 a major crisis over economic policy had developed in West Germany. The impasse in foreign policy aggravated it and demonstrated the general lack of decisiveness of the Erhard government. The solution eventually arrived at was to form a new government based on a coalition in which the Social Democrats replaced the Free Democrats as partners of the Christian Democrats.⁶⁵ Upon the formation of the Grand Coalition under Chancellor Kurt

Georg Kiesinger, distinctly different perceptions and ideas directly influenced the making of foreign policy, since the SPD had never formed part of the government in the whole post-war period. A new direction in the West German approach to East–West relations resulted from the appointment of Willy Brandt, leader of the SPD, as vice-chancellor and foreign minister, and the other leading SPD politician, Herbert Wehner, as minister for all-German affairs.

The official West German stand was now revised, making *détente* and the transformation of East–West relations in Europe necessary preconditions for a solution of the German problem. *Détente* in Europe was no longer described as a threat to primary West German interests, but rather as a stepping-stone to a permanent peaceful order in Europe that would do away with the basic causes of tension in that part of the world. The implications of this change became clear in the first joint declaration of the new government which emphasized its intention to search for peace in Europe by supporting measures of arms control in Central Europe and eliminating political tension.[66] Early in 1967 Foreign Minister Brandt also acknowledged that the European *détente* was something different from, yet dependent on, wider global relaxation of tension between the superpowers. German reunification was now explicitly subordinated to a wider European objective.[67] Not only did the new leadership in Bonn acknowledge that ' German problems ' could be solved only as part of a general settlement in Europe; Mr Brandt even argued that solutions to them could be brought closer ' only after adjustments [had] been made between East and West '. This reversal of the earlier West German position was clearly revealed when he asserted that ' we do not make our policy of *détente* dependent on progress with the German question '.[68] What remained to distinguish the West German position from that of its allies was therefore differences in nuance and emphasis rather than principle. For example, the new West German government was anxious to stress that the relaxation of tension must not be considered as an end in itself but as a means to the ultimate goal of removing the causes of tension and of creating the firm basis for a peaceful and permanent order in Europe.[69]

This idea of a ' just and durable system of peaceful order ' (*Friedensordnung*) was now presented as the objective of its foreign policy. Although the term recurred in many official declarations from the end of 1966 on, its meaning was never clearly defined. The lack of *authoritative* interpretation* was largely due to the fact that the concept served as a compromise formula covering up significant differences of opinion between the two coalition partners on the goals and means for Bonn's relations with the East. As a result politicians of different shadings within the Grand Coalition were not restrained from elaborating their ideas about the proper framework and procedure for a German and European settlement. The following presentation concentrates on the views expressed by Mr Brandt, who in his capacity as foreign minister was the most articulate member of the government on the subject of a future peaceful order in Europe. He himself indicated that his ideas should not be considered as firm proposals but rather as contributions to an on-going debate.[70] The crucial question of the extent to which these ideas were shared by the other members of the government is not easily answered. However, we shall indicate how Mr Brandt's views related to those of his most powerful Cabinet colleagues, Chancellor Kiesinger and the leader of the CSU, Mr Franz Josef Strauss.

Brandt developed two main concepts: a European security system (*Europäisches Sicherheitssystem*) and a European peace order (*Europäische Friedensordnung*). The former he regarded as a stepping-stone to the latter. Each concept has distinct features of its own, as Mr Brandt took pains to explain during 1967 and 1968.

In his view, a workable European security system had to include the renunciation of the use or threat of force among the European states, the balanced reduction of force levels in both parts of Europe and other ' confidence building ' arms control measures in Central Europe, and the participation of both superpowers in the system.[71]

---

*Because of the federal chancellor's constitutional prerogative to determine the main lines of government policy (the so-called *Richtlinienkompetenz*), only interpretations issued or explicitly endorsed by him represent official policy and bind the government.

Mr Brandt indicated that in principle this system could be established in two different ways: by retaining the military alliances and systematically enhancing their peace-stabilizing functions through arms regulations and other measures, or by gradually eliminating NATO and the Warsaw Treaty Organization and replacing them by a new system specially devised to safeguard the security of all European states.[72] Even if the latter course were followed, Mr Brandt emphasized, the active participation of the United States as well as the Soviet Union would be involved.[73] His own preference was for the first method, mainly on the grounds that it would be more practicable.[74]

Upon this system of security the ' durable and just peaceful order in Europe ' could be built. Mr Brandt argued that a true and enduring peace in Europe would require more than the elimination of the danger of war. A genuine East–West reconciliation, particularly between the Federal Republic and the Soviet Union, had to be brought about. That would require nothing less than the mutual adjustment of incompatible goals and positions, which he hoped might eventually be achieved as the result of a lengthy process of gradually expanding areas of co-operation and common interest. Such an approach must include the creation of an institutional framework which would go beyond the nation-state system in Europe. The process of East–West reconciliation would not be completed until the causes of tension on the European continent were eliminated and the split in Europe, showing itself most distinctly in the division of Germany, overcome.[75]

Mr Brandt saw a close connection between the Eastern and Western policies of the Federal Republic and their implications for a future European order. He stressed the importance of an American commitment to any system of peaceful order in Europe [76] and argued that West European unification, far from impeding a reconciliation with the East, would be an element of stability in East–West relations.[77]

The difficulty of establishing Mr Kiesinger's position regarding a future European peace order and the road leading to it flows mainly from the fact that he was less outspoken on this subject than Mr Brandt. We shall limit ourselves to indicating

briefly on which points the views of the Chancellor coincided
with those of his foreign minister and on which points they
seemed to differ.[78]

Kiesinger and Brandt were both convinced that a solution
of the German question could only be achieved through a
transformation of the prevailing European system of confrontation. They also appeared to concur in their preference for
promoting an East–West *rapprochement* through the existing
alliances rather than trying to forge at an early stage a new
security system which could substitute NATO and WTO.[79]
Where they differed was with regard to the *substance* and *timing*
of the ultimate goal of these efforts. To Kiesinger, the solution of the German question meant the reunification of East
and West Germany into a unitary state; in his view, there
could be no European peace order until this goal was realized.[80]
To Brandt, the solution of the German question implied ending
the division of the German nation, a goal which he saw in a
perspective reaching beyond the present nation-state system
to a time when common state boundaries had become much
less relevant. In his concept the establishment of a European
peace order could *precede* the fulfilment of the national aspirations of the German people. He therefore limited himself to
emphasizing that the new European constellation must open
up chances for, or at least not hinder, a settlement of the
German question.[81]

From these diverging views about the ultimate goals of
Bonn's *Deutschlandpolitik* flowed certain differences in their conceptions about proper procedures. While both saw European
and German unification as a long-term process, Kiesinger
seemed more inclined to insist on a close linkage between
measures of East–West *détente* and steps towards German
unity.[82] In addition—and this was a crucial point—his
approach to relations with East Berlin differed from Brandt's.
It is true that both wished to improve contacts with the GDR
leadership in order to make the division less inhuman and
dangerous. But whereas Brandt seemed to regard the communist regime in East Germany—like the other ruling élites
in Eastern Europe—as equal counterparts in any future negotiations on the wider issues of a European and German settlement,

there is nothing to indicate that the Chancellor shared this view. Kiesinger's declarations conveyed the impression that to him the East German leaders remained ' the regime of injustice and oppression ': negotiations had to be conducted with them, on the highest levels of government if necessary, to improve the lot of the East German population and conditions in Berlin; but an arrangement with this regime which would imply a measure of political coexistence seemed unacceptable.[83] These differences in the basic approach to relations with East Germany conferred a distinct ambiguity upon the whole Eastern policy of the Grand Coalition.

The main difference between Mr Brandt's concept and that of Mr Franz Josef Strauss, minister of finance in the government of the Grand Coalition and author of ' a programme for Europe ',[84] was that although both advocated the ' Europeanization ' of the German problem, they approached relations with the East in diametrically opposite fashions. Brandt considered both the Soviet Union and the East European states, at least potentially, as genuine partners in a process of growing co-operation and accommodation, a process which would at first be hampered by the legacies of the past and by mutual suspicion, but one which in the long run would afford the only hope for reconciliation and peace in Europe. His confidence in the ultimate success of this long-range operation was based on the assumption that West European and especially West German economic and technological dynamism could offer the East tangible incentives for co-operation, and that not only the smaller East European states but also the USSR would eventually find it in their own interest to participate in a wider co-operation of this kind, which in time could open up possibilities for some kind of German unification.[85]

Strauss, on the other hand, assumed hostility between the Soviet Union and the West to be a constant factor in world politics. He did not repeat earlier proposals aiming at a ' dismantling ' of communist regimes in Eastern Europe,[86] but in his programme he clearly continued to regard this region as, to begin with, a buffer zone [87] between the Soviet Union and a West European federation, and, at a later stage, as a group of prospective applicants for membership of this federation, which would thus eventually be enlarged to comprise all Europe west of the river Bug.[88] The significant withdrawal of Soviet power implied in this plan would be brought about by the united will of the West European nations to force back Soviet influence, Mr Strauss argued. His scheme also offered two specific incentives to Moscow: the containment of Germany in a federal European state and the loosening of the ties between this autonomous European grouping and the United States.[89] The ' Europeanization ' of the German question, as Strauss used the phrase, thus seemed to mean that the goal of reuniting the German people would become a primary obligation of Germany's West European partners.[90]

This is not the place for a critique of these concepts. The purpose of this brief presentation is to show that both formulas —the European peace order and the pan-European framework for a German settlement—could mean very different things to different people in Bonn.

As a result of Bonn's revised assessment of East–West relations in Europe, West Germany launched in 1967 what has been termed a new *Ostpolitik*. This policy had three main elements: the opening-up of a direct dialogue with Moscow, the search for full normalization of relations with the East European states between the Bug and Oder rivers, and the achievement of a *modus vivendi* with East Germany without recognizing the GDR as a separate state. One of the first moves Mr Brandt undertook after assuming the post of foreign minister was to suggest a confidential exchange of views with the Soviet Union on a whole list of problems, with an agreement on the renunciation of the use of force as the central issue.[91] The efforts to remove obstacles to a reconciliation with the other East European states were primarily reflected in the decision to abandon the earlier narrow interpretation of the Hallstein doctrine in order to clear the way for full diplomatic relations with all the communist states in Eastern Europe, and thus avoid a situation in which the German nation would be represented in these countries solely by GDR diplomats.[92] In addition, Bonn did not repeat its contention that the borders of 1937 constituted the legal basis for negotiation about a final settlement in Central Europe. East Germany was now included explicitly in the efforts to improve relations with the East, which meant that the former policy of isolating the Pankow regime had been abandoned. By recognizing the *existence* of a second political system on German soil through the extension of official contacts with East German authorities, Bonn sought to diminish the hostility in intra-German relations gradually, to alleviate some of the hardships of the division, and thereby to halt the process of alienation between the two parts of Germany.[93] However, as indicated above, the ultimate goal remained ambiguous because of conflicting views within the Grand Coalition.

To sum up, the new West German government had come to the conclusion that it was necessary to adapt its policy to the general trend in Western policy. It remained somewhat less confident than its main allies in Europe about the nature of the European *détente*, but it was determined to use whatever relaxation there was to try to reach an understanding with the East. Because Bonn continued to be singled out by the Soviet Union as the main saboteur of a European settlement, it was anxious to get the full backing of the Western allies for its new policy.[94] At the same time, however, the Federal Republic began to display a measure of independent initiative in the field of East–West relations that hardly had any counterpart in West German foreign policy during the post-war era. This seems to have been due partly to the concern of the leadership in Bonn to break the deadlock on the Central European issues, and partly to a trend towards German self-assertion, which Willy Brandt depicted as a necessary element in the process of national recuperation.[95]

The scope for consensus and the problems of policy co-ordination

Having examined the official views and policies of the main Western powers as they evolved during the period 1966–8, it remains to identify the scope for consensus by determining the degree of similarity in their views and by examining some of the problems of policy co-ordination. Common to all the Western governments included in this study was the fact that they attributed the European *détente* to a basic change in Soviet conduct. Where official opinion differed was with regard to the main reasons for this change. The following four were generally referred to in official declarations and comments:

1. The trend towards fragmentation in the Soviet alliance, most marked by the Sino–Soviet split.

2. Internal developments in the Soviet Union, which tended on the whole to make it more in the interest of the political élite to maintain a low level of international tension.

3. The success of the Western alliance in containing Soviet expansionism.

4. The nuclear stalemate between the superpowers. [96]

The United States usually put most emphasis on the significance of the last two factors. [97] The same holds true for West Germany until the fall of the Erhard government. From early 1967 until August 1968 all four factors were given roughly equal consideration in West German statements, and in British as well. France emphasized the first two factors almost to the exclusion of the other two, or, in any case, of the third factor.

The reasons for these differences in stress were related first to the relative importance of East–West relations in Europe in each country's foreign policy as a whole, and then to the priorities they each gave to the various elements of their relations with the East. As for the former, distinctions can be made between the position of the United States and of Western Europe, as well as between Britain and the continental states.

In the United States developments after the bombing of North Vietnam began in 1965 led to increasing concentration of public attention and material resources on problems in South-East Asia. Moreover, the efforts of the American government continued to be directed to meeting the global challenge of the Soviet Union, yet managing with Moscow's co-operation the problems they shared as nuclear superpowers. In this situation, the natural American inclination was to view East–West relations in Europe as subordinate to these primary concerns.

In the three leading West European states, East–West relations were no longer perceived primarily as a common problem of defence and deterrence but more and more as an important factor determining the future configuration of forces both in Europe as a whole and in the more immediately relevant context of West European power politics. In the case of West Germany and France, the evolution of East–West relations was directly linked up with the avowed national preoccupations of these two countries: the solution of the German question, and the rise of France to a position of pre-eminence in a reconstituted Europe, respectively. For Britain, on the other hand, relations with the Soviet Union and Eastern Europe only indirectly affected the policy issues that were of most immediate concern to the government in London: opening up the road to Europe and repairing the British economy.

The relative importance of East–West relations in Europe in the over-all spectrum of policy issues confronting each of the Western governments was of course closely related to their respective preferences for alternative European constellations and certain lines of policy to achieve them.

The overriding preoccupation of the United States in the development of East–West relations in Europe was the control of conflict and the stability of the European politico-military environment. Attributing priority to measures that would preserve—and if possible enhance—stability did not necessarily imply accepting the *status quo* in Europe as compatible with basic American national interests. It could be argued, however, that the acceptance of the *status quo* as the basis for a European settlement conflicted with fundamental American interests only to the extent that the prevailing situation in Central Europe was perceived as inherently unstable. Thus, while the policy of ' peaceful engagement ' in Eastern Europe was explained by American officials as a strategy to bring about a new political environment conducive to the settlement of unresolved issues in Central Europe, the main consideration of decision-makers in Washington in connection with the choice of this policy may very well have been the *control* rather than the resolution of conflict. A proposed line of action which held out some prospect for gradual peaceful change may have appeared the best way to contain the political forces that could jeopardize the relative stability which had been

achieved in that sensitive area.[98]   A consequence of this was
the inclination in Washington to emphasize the importance of
NATO (or at least the Atlantic alliance) not only as an essential
fall-back position, but also as a framework for the continued
search for East–West *rapprochement* in Europe.[99]

Britain like the United States favoured the Atlantic framework, and for similar reasons.   Ambivalence about her role in
the world and the difficulties of finding a way into Europe
made NATO appear to be an indispensable element of stability.
It would not only maintain American presence on the European
continent to balance the strength of the Soviet Union, but also
assure Britain a place of influence in the Western family of
nations.   At the same time, the pressure to think about solutions to the intractable German problem was not felt with any
great urgency, and the preoccupation with achieving a sustained recovery and growth of the British economy predisposed
London to favour measures that would allow the reduction of
force levels on the European continent.   Thus the emphasis
with regard to the future of East–West relations was on lowering the risks and costs of the Central European confrontation
through arms control measures.   Although the governments of
all Western countries had come to subscribe to the notion
that *détente* was a necessary precondition for a European settlement, it was for Britain, more than for the two main continental
powers, also an end in itself.

West Germany's position was complex.   On the one hand,
due to her exposed situation the Federal Republic had to be as
interested as any of her main allies in the aspect of Western
policy which emphasized *control* of conflict.   On the other hand,
it was only through the *resolution* of basic conflict issues in Central
Europe—or at least significant developments leading in that
direction—that she could hope to attain the main national goal
of the German people: some form of unification between East
and West Germany.   What every government in Bonn had to
guard against was the pursuit of one of these aims at the expense
of the other.[100]   The West German government was confronted
with a special dilemma; it had to accept the *status quo* in Europe
to reassure the East—and yet it must strive for a transformation
of conditions in Central Europe in order to overcome the

division of the German people.[101]   Once the relaxation of tension was no longer regarded by Bonn as a bargain-counter for steps towards reunification but as a necessary element in a policy aiming to solve the German question, the long-suppressed, genuine West German interest in stabilizing the military environment in Central Europe could come into play.   That facilitated the emergence of a basic consensus between Washington, London, and Bonn on the desirability of promoting *détente* by arms regulations in Central Europe.

France's preoccupation with improvement of her status and the restoration of Europe to a position of greater independence from the superpowers militated against her consenting to any measures that could be construed as acceptance of the prevailing *status quo*.   Consequently, while France was interested in arms limitation in Central Europe as an instrument of rank differentiation between herself and Germany, she opposed arms control schemes that would be based on the existing military alliances.   This position was facilitated by her geographical situation, which enabled her to leave the problem of conflict control largely to her Western partners (except in Berlin, where France's status as one of the Big Four was involved) and to concentrate on other aspects of East–West relations, mainly the cultivation of bilateral contacts with individual East European countries.   A settlement in Central Europe was seen in Paris as a primary French interest not because of any special desire to have a united Germany of eighty million people as a neighbour (although the French government, like all Western governments, has paid lip-service to the cause of German unification), but because only a solution of the German problem would permit the definite elimination of superpower predominance and thus the emergence of a reconstituted, independent Europe.

The ' Europeanization ' of the German question was a common characteristic of French and West German programmes for peace in Europe, yet the differences in the two concepts were more striking than their similarity.   Not only were future relations with the United States conceived differently; two other features were of equal, if not greater, significance.

Firstly, while General de Gaulle saw the emergence of a new Europe as a consequence of the reassertion of the individuality of European nations and states, the West German concept was predicated on the erosion of national borders and the creation of structures wider than the existing nation-state system for the growth of pan-European identity and allegiance.

Secondly, whereas both the French and the West German programmes aimed at a rise in rank for their respective countries, there was a difference not only in the status to which they aspired but also in the procedure envisaged. De Gaulle wished to restore France to the status of a great power—at least in terms of preserving a margin between the victors of World War II and the losers—but no post-war government in West Germany had ever entertained great-power ambitions. [102] However, de Gaulle was also anxious to establish France's status within a future European peace order higher than Germany's, and at the earliest possible time. France's higher rank would be assured by its nuclear arsenal and its role as ' co-guarantor ' of the new European order. The West German concept, on the other hand, appeared to imply an unwillingness to anticipate and predetermine the status of any West European member in a future pan-European order. This was partly a result of the ' beyond the nation-state ' perspective prevailing in West German official thinking. In addition, statements from Bonn indicated that officials were unwilling to yield to French demands because they expected that Germany's rank relative to France would improve in the long run as a consequence of its economic dynamism. [103]

Because of these differences in outlook and priorities, the problems of policy co-ordination within the Atlantic alliance were exceedingly difficult. In essence, what could be achieved was some agreement on the management of relations with the East that did not prejudge the ultimate result of the on-going *rapprochement* between East and West. In view of the generally felt need to reassess the balance between the defensive and the political functions of the Atlantic alliance, a committee was set up under the Belgian foreign minister, Pierre Harmel, to study its future tasks. In the committee's final report, the role of the alliance in promoting *détente* was considered to be largely that of a clearing-house through which the member-states could co-ordinate their efforts to improve relations with the East. Rather than making concrete suggestions for a Western peace programme, the report sought to ensure a minimum consonance in the pursuit of *détente* policies and to emphasize the importance of Alliance cohesion for their success.[104] The redefinition of West Germany's foreign policy made it easier for all participants in the Harmel committee to agree on very general long-range goals in terms less rigid than those that had been customary for NATO statements. Nevertheless, those sections of the final report which dealt with actions that the allies might take in common to promote these ultimate objectives were vague and they reflected differences between the multilateral approach favoured by the Atlanticists and the bilateral one insisted upon by France.[105]

By the spring of 1968 the Western allies demonstrated their concurring views with regard to the *immediate* steps on the road towards further East–West *détente* at the regular ministerial meeting of the North Atlantic Council. At this session, the Council adopted a declaration that proposed a gradual, balanced lowering of force levels, particularly in Central Europe. It concluded with a call to the Soviet Union and the other East European countries ' to join in this search for progress towards peace '.[106] However, this appeal became meaningless for the immediate future, when, less than two months later, the Soviet Union in a dramatic way strengthened her military presence in the heart of Europe by occupying Czechoslovakia.

THE EAST AND THE EUROPEAN
DÉTENTE, 1966–1968

THE analyst of official Soviet and East European declarations is confronted with special problems of interpretation that arise as a result of the doctrinal underpinning of communist policy statements and the ideological ties between the ruling élites in the socialist countries. To define the international situation in accordance with the predetermined stages in the historical process foreseen in Marxist theory has a distinct operational significance in the policy-making process of these countries.

As noted above, the official view of a given situation is always to some extent related to preferred policy choices. It would seem justified, however, to assume a closer linkage in the East than in the West. Policy-makers in the socialist countries operate under conditions that are in many respects different from those prevailing in the West. Two in particular are important here. On the one hand, the ruling élites in the East subscribe to an ideology that preaches 'the unity of theory and action', a factor conducive to establishing an especially close link between official descriptions of the world situation and concrete prescriptions for action. On the other hand, policy-makers in communist states enjoy far greater freedom to formulate and publicize their perceptions of the international situation in accordance with their preconceived preferences, since they need not fear nearly as much as their Western colleagues being challenged in these assessments by independent centres of public information within their own societies. One could argue therefore that when the leaders of socialist countries define the state of international affairs, by so doing they often actually reflect decisions to pursue certain concrete policies.

The common ideological background of the ruling élites in socialist countries creates obvious pressures to conform in out-look and assessment. Consequently, official Soviet and East

European descriptions of the world situation tend to be rather stereotyped. As a general rule differences in the assessments of the various governments can only be inferred from hints and omissions. Nevertheless, the standard Eastern description of the European situation has been sufficiently ambiguous during recent years to give certain East European countries some leeway in choosing their foreign policy, leeway they have not failed to exploit. The scrutiny of what Moscow and its East European allies perceive as preferred *lines of action* is therefore likely to bring out a slightly more complex picture of Eastern views of European developments, their requirements, and their potentialities than the standard descriptions would provide.

These national preferences of the ruling groups in the Soviet Union and the individual East European states must be seen against the background of their domestic preoccupations, and in order to identify them it is also necessary to acquaint ourselves with the positions collectively agreed upon within the Soviet alliance at Bucharest in July 1966 and at Karlovy Vary in April 1967.

Domestic trends in the Soviet alliance during the 1960s[1]

By the middle of the 1960s the ruling élites in Moscow and the capitals of the East European states faced similar problems concerning the fundamental issue of how to transform a highly centralized command economy to a system of economic planning and management better suited to meeting the requirements of a maturing industrial society. A fall in the growth rates of these countries and a rise in the effective consumer demand that the economies were unable to satisfy indicated that changes were necessary. A common feature of all the different reforms that were discussed and cautiously implemented in some of these countries was a devolution of decision-making powers from the party bureaucrats and their administrative assistants to professionals who, though communists, were primarily devoted to technical and economic efficiency. These changes in the management and further development of the socialist societies in Eastern Europe could not be implemented without major modifications in their power structure. Already a managerial group, with its own *esprit de corps*, had begun to form. Furthermore, since these new economic systems were designed to satisfy the requirements and preferences of the many groups whose voluntary co-operation is needed for a complex industrial society to run smoothly, they implied far greater participation by large segments of the population in a wide range of public activities than had been the case before. Even though the ruling élites in most of the East European countries and the Soviet Union were aware of the need to transform the economic patterns of the 1950s, they were clearly concerned about the political repercussions of any major change. The basic dilemma of the rulers in the more advanced countries—the Soviet Union, Czechoslovakia, East Germany, and Hungary—was that they could not let the economic apparatus grind to a halt, yet they were anxious about the political consequences of the economic reforms, to which they saw no genuine alternative.

The responses of the leaders differed, depending on the specific circumstances of each country, but there was some general similarity. A common initial reaction was to try to protect the traditional structure of political authority and control from the onslaught of the economic pragmatists without explicitly challenging their substantive proposals. In time it became more and more difficult to do this because of the inherent linkage between effective economic reforms and changes in the political superstructure, and other remedies had to be found.

In Czechoslovakia the regime under Antonin Novotny overtly acknowledged the need for basic changes, and initially showed a measure of boldness in initiating them. But in the course of 1966 and 1967 the top leaders became increasingly unwilling to implement the recommendations of the reformers working under Professor Ota Sik. In the last analysis, this meant that the party leadership preferred economic stagnation to risking innovations that could jeopardize its power position. However, Novotny's strategy of inertia proved to be no solution, for a severe crisis developed, and he was forced to resign.

In East Germany during the mid-1960s the situation was different, partly because of the generally more repressive political climate and partly because of the comparatively large number of professionals who held important positions within the party, which enabled it to institute important economic and administrative reforms itself.

Only the Czechoslovak leadership under Mr Novotny's successor, Alexander Dubcek—and, of course, the Yugoslav party leaders (whose ideas and measures are not included in this brief review)—arrived at the conclusion that the requirements of an advanced socialist society called for a totally new conception of the role of the communist party. Among the other East European communist leaders, the Hungarians under Mr Janos Kadar came closest to this position. Like the Czechoslovaks after January 1968—and unlike the East Germans—the Hungarian leadership explicitly acknowledged the need for political changes to accompany the introduction of a new economic system.[2] They attempted to prevent major institutional changes and to contain the trend towards an erosion of the party's monopoly of power by ensuring close and continuous party control over the whole process of transformation. Indeed, Hungary may yet turn out to be the socialist country where the leaders manage most successfully to internalize the growing influence of the technocrats within the ranks of the governing party.

In the Soviet Union, the collective leadership under Brezhnev and Kosygin had difficulty in coping with the strains on bureaucratic centralism, which they wished to preserve as a basic feature of the political system. Both the party and state bureaucracies had been exposed to major shocks as a result of Nikita Khrushchev's improvisations. They had only begun to recover and were resisting further reorganization. Nevertheless, the professional economists continued to point out the need for streamlining the administrative structure. In addition, the new leadership was confronted with an upsurge of criticism from Soviet intellectuals who directed their attacks against party bureaucrats discredited by their Stalinist past. The main responses of the collective leadership in Moscow to these pressures could be seen in a series of repressive measures in all fields of cultural activity, an insistence on ideological conformity, and an increased emphasis on social discipline and patriotism.

The various initiatives taken by the East European countries were therefore doubly unwelcome to the Soviet leaders. Since communication between professional people in the Soviet Union and countries allied to it was close (especially amongst economists), the new ideas contributed to the dissatisfaction of important groups within the USSR and ultimately challenged the rulers in the Kremlin within their own domestic environment. To a certain extent, the Soviet leaders could count on the co-operation of the ruling élites in Eastern Europe to handle their domestic problems in accordance with Moscow's wishes, for they shared with them the common concern about the conflicting requirements of rational economic management and effective party rule. On the other hand, however, the call for reform in Hungary, Czechoslovakia, and East Germany brought forward somewhat different solutions, thereby strengthening the force of nationalism, an undercurrent in all East European states, and making developments in the Soviet alliance less susceptible to Moscow's control. In Rumania the nationalist feeling was particularly strong and found expression more in foreign policy initiatives than in domestic change. It was also on the rise in Poland where the Minister of Internal Affairs, General Mieczyslaw Moczar, was its most powerful proponent. Whatever the motivation for emphasizing the importance of different roads to socialism in each country, it is clear that Moscow's allies were cultivating their own national interests and developing the self-confidence to assert them. This would hardly have been possible had it not been for the existence of the Sino–Soviet split and the relaxation in East–West relations in Europe, both of which tended to increase the relative freedom of action of the East European states. As it was, they could develop bilateral ties with Western countries and, within certain limits, differentiate their attitudes towards the West. Soviet reactions to the European *détente* clearly reflected Moscow's concern to counteract these repercussions within its own camp.

Détente 1966: Soviet and Rumanian versions

The document which set the tone for official Soviet foreign policy views during this period was that part of the Central

Committee Report to the 23rd Congress of the Communist
Party of the Soviet Union which dealt with the international
situation. The Congress assembled in March 1966 at a time
when the Soviet leadership appeared to be reassessing some of
its assumptions about the character and trend of East–West
relations in the light of the intensified Vietnamese conflict.
Towards the United States the Soviet leaders were inclined to
continue their adversary–partner relationship—which had
permitted mutual tacit restraint and even limited co-operation
in spite of fundamental differences—but they now put more
stress on the adversary aspect than before. One can see that
they were becoming more concerned about the growth of
American military power and assertiveness and more aware
of the opportunities opening up throughout the world, and
especially in some West European countries, as a result of the
growing opposition to American intervention in Vietnam.
The conclusions the Soviet leadership drew from these observations at the 23rd Party Congress were tentative, but they
suggested that Moscow was adopting a *differentiated approach
towards the West*: a hardening of its attitude to the United States,
and, at the same time, a continued, or even stepped-up, *détente*
policy towards Western Europe with the exception of West
Germany.[3]

Mr Brezhnev's report described the period since the previous
Party Congress as being characterized by:

a constant increase in the international influence of the Soviet
Union and of the entire world system of Socialism; by fresh victories
of the countries and peoples who are fighting against colonial
oppression for their independence and progress; by activation of
the struggle of the working class in the capitalist countries and the
further development of the international Communist and workers'
movement.

Against these hopeful developments the report set the gloomy
picture of ' the deepening of the general crisis of capitalism
and the growth of contradictions between the capitalist
countries ' leading to ' insolent and provocative actions, even
including military adventures '. While the increased aggressiveness of imperialism was not seen as an indication of a change
in the over-all balance of forces in favour of imperialism, but

rather as a sign of its desperation, the report nevertheless concluded that ' *the international situation has been aggravated* '.[4]

Official Soviet descriptions of world events during this period usually mentioned these two main trends in international politics: on the one hand, the growing power and influence of the world system of socialist states and its actual or potential allies in the capitalist countries and the Third World, and on the other hand, the increasing aggressiveness of imperialism as the crisis of capitalism became ever more aggravated. No explicit priority was accorded to either of these tendencies, but in general, representative Soviet statements during 1966 conveyed the impression that the latter was of more immediate concern in Moscow. One can note an unmistakable inclination to emphasize the dangers of the prevailing situation, not least in Europe, where the alleged revanchist designs of West German militarists were portrayed as part and parcel of an intensification in the aggressive activities of imperialism.[5] Given the basic communist contention that international tensions are mainly a result of the existence of the capitalist system, the trend towards *détente* in Europe was described by the Soviet leadership mainly in terms of the growing strength of the ' peace forces ' and the erosion of American influence in Western Europe.[6]

The ambiguity contained in this double image of world affairs did not prevent Moscow from drawing forthright conclusions about the policies that were required of the socialist states under the prevailing circumstances. First and foremost stood the consolidation of the socialist camp, or, to use the official Soviet language, the need to strengthen ' the fraternal cooperation of the socialist states ' and to promote ' the further coordination and effectiveness of their foreign policy actions '.[7] This policy prescription was put forward primarily as a measure to counter the imperialist threat. But it was also argued that the East European countries would have to be a cohesive unit if they were to succeed in exploiting the opportunities opening up in Western Europe—by forming an anti-imperialist front with progressive forces there.[8] A second policy conclusion implied in these official Soviet descriptions of the international scene was more directly addressed to the fact that the ' progressive ' elements in the bourgeois camp had become more active and assertive. Here the basic notion was that the Soviet Union should, in the words of Foreign Minister Andrei Gromyko, ' raise problems that have become ripe and strive for their solution, relying on the support of the peoples, on the support of all peace-loving forces '.[9] This seemed to foreshadow new Soviet initiatives for solving the German problem and safeguarding European security. It also suggested that Moscow would step up its efforts to split the Western alliance.

The Soviet view of the European *détente* in 1966 was therefore that the capitalist countries were beginning to be at odds with one another, as was inevitable, and that the position of ' peace-loving forces' in Western Europe was strengthened. This meant that the dangers of irrational aggression from the West were greater, but so were the opportunities for making gains, especially with the United States distracted by other problems. The course of action called for in either case was to strengthen the unity of the communist movement in Europe.

One particular way of consolidating the socialist camp was to tighten up the Warsaw Treaty Organization. Moscow had stressed this point earlier and most explicitly in September 1965 when Mr Brezhnev called for the further perfecting of the WTO and suggested the creation of ' permanent and prompt machinery for considering pressing problems '.[10] The reactions of the East European leaders to these Soviet initiatives were hardly encouraging. At the 23rd Congress of the CPSU, however, the Soviet leadership reasserted its intention of strengthening co-operation with the other socialist countries within the framework of the Warsaw Pact.[11] Shortly afterwards, the General Secretary of the Rumanian communist party, Mr Nicolae Ceausescu, retorted with a condemnation of military blocs that clearly revealed an important difference of opinion between him and the Soviet leaders.[12]

Mr Ceausescu's view of the international scene coincided with the official Soviet view in so far as it reflected the concept of intensified imperialist activity in an over-all situation favouring the socialist countries. But whereas the Soviet Union had tried to establish a close relation between United

States aggression in Vietnam and the ' revanchist ' designs of West German militarists, there was a conspicuous absence of such linkage in Mr Ceausescu's declaration. The only example of intensified imperialist aggression in addition to Vietnam that he cited was the bloody repression of the communist party in Indonesia. With regard to Europe, the views of the Rumanian party leader seem to have been determined by his firm conviction that the activities of individual nations and states were of primary importance for the development and safeguarding of peace and prosperity. This led him to emphasize the significance of a free development of economic, cultural, scientific, and political ties between all countries, irrespective of their social systems.

As for the need to increase the vigilance of the socialist camp in the face of intensified imperialist aggressiveness, the Rumanian leadership maintained that the best way to strengthen the world system of socialist states was to let each of them develop its resources in fraternal co-operation with the other members of the camp. Thus, while heeding the Soviet call for the solidarity of all anti-imperialist forces, the Rumanian leadership showed little interest in Moscow's insistence on strengthening *military* preparedness. In a speech in June 1966, Mr Ceausescu emphasized that Rumania intended to increase her fighting power and defensive strength primarily by developing her economy.[13] The Warsaw Treaty Organization itself, according to the contention of the Rumanian leader, was needed only so long as the socialist countries in Europe were confronted by the ' aggressive Atlantic Pact '.

It is in that perspective that Ceausescu renewed Rumania's demand for the liquidation of military blocs and bases and for the withdrawal of all troops from the territory of other states, phenomena which he described as major obstacles to the free development of co-operation between nations. In comparison with the high priority ascribed to these policy recommendations, the call (emphatically repeated in Soviet declarations) to recognize the realities of the situation in Central Europe and to prevent West German ' revanchists ' from getting access to nuclear weapons sounded far less urgent.[14] Thus, his list of priorities was almost the inverse of that of the Sovie leaders.

The Soviet–Rumanian dialogue that ensued, the heat of which can at least partly be traced in the public records,[15] eventually led to a compromise at the meeting of the Political Consultative Committee of the Warsaw Treaty member-states in Bucharest in July 1966.

The Bucharest Declaration of 1966

In early June 1966 it was not at all certain that a declaration on European security would be issued at the forthcoming meeting of the Political Consultative Committee of the WTO in Bucharest. The Soviet Union had made it clear that it wished to issue such a declaration, but objections were raised by Rumania. These were overcome after a rather lengthy airing of differences, but the difficulty in forming a consensus showed up in the inconsistencies that can be found in the actual text of the Declaration, issued on 6 July 1966.

The general description of the state of world affairs again centred around the two main trends encountered in all major foreign policy declarations emanating from socialist countries during this period: ' the peaceful and the aggressive ', to use the shorthand definition of Andrei Gromyko.[16] As in earlier communist statements, no predominance was ascribed to either tendency,[17] but both were presented in a somewhat modified manner and with slightly different policy conclusions from those in previous Soviet declarations.

The communist leaders assembled at Bucharest established a very close link between United States ' aggression ' in Vietnam and the danger to peace in Europe when they declared that

a direct peril to peace in Europe, to the security of European peoples is spelled by the present policy of the United States of America which, in another region of the world—in South-East Asia—has led to the unleashing of an aggressive war against the Vietnamese people.[18]

This formulation was in clear contrast to the inclination of Rumania (and possibly other East European countries) to view the situation in Europe as basically peaceful. On the other hand, the conference reached the conclusion that in Europe ' the possibility exists of preventing a course of events unwished for '. Conditions thus appeared to be ripe for joint action by all ' progressive ' forces in order to solve the problems of European security. On balance, it would seem that the Bucharest Declaration brought into sharper focus both the *dangers* and the *opportunities* of the European situation.

In terms of *policy implications* the meeting arrived at the following three main conclusions:

1. It legitimized the further development of ' a system of ties among peoples and of inter-state relations ' between Eastern and Western Europe without raising demands for prior fulfilment of specific conditions on the part of West European countries, such as the recognition of East Germany or of existing frontiers in Central Europe.

2. It issued a call for the mobilization of ' anti-imperialist forces ' in Western Europe in the name of European peace and security.

3. It renewed an earlier proposal for the concomitant abolition of NATO and the Warsaw Treaty Organization and the establishment of a European security system.

The specific wording of these three points in the Declaration reflected the fact that the agreement reached at Bucharest was based on a number of compromises between the Soviet Union and her East European allies. Each of them requires some further elaboration.

The need for the expansion of ' good neighbourly relations ' among all European states seems to have been more an East European than a Soviet concern since the more developed of these countries were anxious to modernize their societies with the help of West European capital and technological know-how.[19] The primary Soviet concern must have been to prevent the growth of pan-European co-operation from eroding Moscow's political influence in Eastern Europe. These partly conflicting interests can be traced in the text of the Declaration. Thus, in the action programme, although the list of specific areas in which co-operation might be developed conspicuously omitted the political one, the concluding statement, that ' there is no domain of peaceful co-operation where the European states could not find opportunities for further, mutually beneficial steps ', implicitly incorporated political

E

co-operation as well. An earlier section of the Declaration dealing with general principles stressed the importance of ' the strengthening of political relations between states irrespective of their social system ', but added the modifying phrase, ' relations aimed at defending peace ', which only papered over the inherent differences. A final point is that while the Declaration did not stipulate any preconditions for the development of co-operative ties between Eastern and Western Europe, it did include the following general principle:

Development of general European cooperation requires that all states should renounce any kind of discrimination and pressure, political or economic, in relation to other countries, should co-operate on an equal footing and should establish normal relations between them, inclusive of the establishment of normal relations with both Germanys.

It seems that the Soviet Union and East Germany intended this principle to check the growth of East European contacts with West Germany, but the wording was sufficiently vague for Rumania to be able to establish full diplomatic relations with West Germany in early 1967 and even to argue that its action was compatible with the position adopted at Bucharest.

The call to mobilize an ' anti-imperialist ' front in Western Europe, with its distinct anti-American overtones, represented a Soviet rather than an East European concern.[20] Here again, the Bucharest Declaration was formulated in a way that indicated that a compromise was reached. On the one hand, it strongly condemned United States policy in Europe, which was said to have ' nothing in common with the vital interests of the European peoples '. It also stressed that the European states were ' in a position to solve the problems of their mutual relationship without interference from the outside '. On the other hand, the action programme of the Declaration proposed that a conference on European security and co-operation be convened, an idea especially cherished by the Polish leaders since 1964.[21] With regard to the composition of that conference, it was stated that no exceptions were made by the Warsaw Treaty states about which countries should participate in such deliberations. This formulation was one degree more ambiguous than Moscow's standard phrases on the subject, which suggests that some adjustment was made to the preferences of its East European allies.[22]

Since the Rumanian leaders had argued that the existence of military blocs represented an obstacle to co-operation between states, the inclusion in the action programme of a proposal to eliminate NATO and the WTO phrased in these terms signified that the Rumanian point of view had substantial support at the conference. On the other hand, the Declaration emphasized the need to strengthen the defensive capacity of the members of the Warsaw Treaty as long as the North Atlantic bloc existed and the aggressive, imperialist circles disrupted peace the world over.* And while the formula used in this connection was not the one preferred by Moscow, it nevertheless could be used in support of Soviet demands for ' perfecting the mechanism ' of the Warsaw Treaty Organization as such.[23]

The follow-up each member of the Soviet alliance accorded the Bucharest Declaration reflected their special concerns. Thus, the encouragement the Declaration gave to further development of co-operation with Western European countries was of most immediate importance to Rumania, which used it as grounds for speeding up the negotiations with West Germany that eventually led to the establishment of full diplomatic relations between Bucharest and Bonn.

The East German leader, Walter Ulbricht, emphasized the principle incorporated in the Declaration that pan-European co-operation and the normalization of inter-state relations between East and West required the establishment of normal relations with the German Democratic Republic. In his opinion the renunciation by West Germany of its claim to represent all of Germany was the cardinal test for the relaxation of tension in Europe. As long as that was not forthcoming Mr Ulbricht was apparently unwilling to acknowledge the existence of any kind of *détente*.[24]

In Poland the governing élite seems to have been anxious to emphasize that the development of Polish–West German

---

*It is worth noting that by relating the continued need for the WTO not only to the existence of NATO, as before, but also to the vaguer notion of a ' global imperialist threat ', Moscow seems to have been hedging against the remote possibility of the dissolution of NATO.

co-operation in economic and commercial fields presupposed certain political concessions on the part of the Federal Republic.[25] As to the appeal of the Bucharest conference to mobilize the ' anti-imperialist forces ' in Western Europe, the Polish leadership sought to implement these directives by cultivating Poland's traditionally good relations with France. Thus, on his return from the Bucharest conference the First Secretary of the Central Committee of the Polish Workers' party, Wladyslaw Gomulka, spoke approvingly of those ' governing circles of Western Europe, which, guided by realism and in the name of their own interests, want to free themselves from the hegemony of the United States and to pursue a more independent policy '. He asserted that ' realization of the aspirations of the West European countries and particularly those of France for greater independence, thus coincides with the aims of socialist countries to ease tensions and dispel the threat of armed conflict in Europe'.[26]

The Soviet follow-up to the Bucharest Declaration consisted of a statement re-emphasizing the identity of purpose between American ' imperialism ' and West German ' revanchism '. In the Soviet view therefore, ' European security ' still depended on the success of the ' peace-loving forces in breaking the ignominious " axis " Washington–Bonn '.[27] Consequently, Moscow directed an appeal to the wavering Erhard government in West Germany, urging it to renounce its ' collusion with the aggressive circles of the USA ' and its support of ' revanchist forces ' within the Federal Republic.[28] In a strikingly conciliatory tone, *Pravda*, the main organ of the communist party of the Soviet Union, asserted on 21 September 1966:

We understand how difficult this choice is for Bonn. However, this is no cause for malicious glee. If the responsible figures of the Federal Republic of Germany would muster their courage and recognize the groundlessness of their entire post-war political conception, no one in Europe would gloat over them.

And this was followed by a hint of what Moscow was in a position to offer as remuneration for a change of course on the part of West Germany:

Objectively speaking, the German people could derive more benefit than any people of Europe from the development of all-European cooperation. For them it is not only a question of ensuring their own security and vitally important economic ties, but also a question of searches for approaches to the solution to the national problem.[29]

There was in these pronouncements, however, no indication of any change in the basic Soviet position on the Central European issues, which demanded the recognition of the *status quo* on the part of the Federal Republic as the first step towards East–West reconciliation in Europe.

The Soviet declarations suggesting an attempt to pry West Germany away from its Atlantic orientation were later supplemented with denunciations of American ' bridge-building ' efforts in Europe. The Johnson administration's concern to revitalize American policy towards Europe by lending support to the idea of European reconciliation induced the Soviet party leader, Mr Brezhnev, to characterize President Johnson as the ' uninvited manager of European affairs '.[30] Thus, the main thrust of Moscow's policy towards Western Europe appeared to be directed as before at breaking, or at least loosening up, the crucial American–West German link, the backbone of the military alliance confronting the Soviet Union in Europe.

To sum up, the European situation and its potentialities reflected in the Bucharest Declaration centred around two main concerns: (a) the *consolidation* of the *status quo*, and (b) the *exploitation of new opportunities* opening up in the more fluid situation of the late 1960s.

Different priorities and goals seem to have been associated with these two purposes by the Soviet Union on the one hand and most East European states on the other. To Moscow, consolidation of the *status quo* meant both the fixation of the dividing line in Central Europe and the preservation of its hegemonic position in Eastern Europe. To the East European leaders (with the exception of Mr Ulbricht, for whom dependence on Soviet presence and support remained crucial, although perhaps less so than earlier), the fixation of existing border lines in Central Europe was important exactly because it could facilitate the loosening of Moscow's grip over Eastern Europe. Similarly, different aspirations were implicated in the wish to exploit the opportunities opening up in Western Europe. To the Soviet Union, the situation seemed to afford a chance to promote a further significant fragmentation of the Western alliance. The East European countries, on the other hand, hoped to use the Soviet endorsement of East–West co-operation to develop ties with the technologically advanced and economically dynamic states of Western Europe willing to provide urgently needed help to stimulate the East European economies. With the changing of the guard in Bonn at the end of 1966 and the new *Ostpolitik* initiated by the West German coalition government, these differences soon became more sharply exposed.

The impact of West Germany's new Ostpolitik

The change of course inaugurated by the new government of the Grand Coalition in Bonn added significantly to the disarray in the Soviet camp, which had up to then been revealed most clearly by Rumania's independent stand and intransigence towards Moscow.

The earliest unambiguous Eastern reaction to the foreign policy pronouncements of the Kiesinger–Brandt government came from East Berlin. In line with the general hardening of the East German attitude towards Bonn from the summer of 1966 on,[31] this reaction was emphatically negative. In December 1966, shortly after the publication of the main guidelines for the policy of the new government in Bonn, Walter Ulbricht denounced the programme of the Kiesinger government as ' revanchist ' in foreign policy and ' anti-democratic ' in domestic matters, and depicted Bonn's ' new ' course as an attempt to escape from isolation by tactical manoeuvres, which in his view were doomed beforehand due to the insincerity of the whole enterprise and the inadequacy of the proposed measures. Mr Ulbricht was especially critical of the offer made by the new West German government to exchange declarations with individual East European governments on the renunciation of the use of force in settling disputes between the contracting parties, including the issue of Germany's division. The latter was construed by the East German leader as a clumsy attempt to elicit from the East European governments the indirect legalization of Bonn's ' revanchist ' claim of sole representation.[32] Diplomatic representations of the East German authorities in East European capitals during January 1967 indicated that this point was of major concern to the East German leadership. From this issue subsequently evolved what was often termed the *Ulbricht doctrine* (or the inverted Hallstein doctrine), namely the formal East German demand that recognition of the GDR by the Federal Republic should be made the precondition of the establishment of full diplomatic relations between any East European state and the Federal Republic. Thus, while according to official East German statements no basic change had occurred in the European situation as a consequence of developments in Bonn, East Berlin soon became sufficiently agitated to issue explicit warnings to its allies about the machinations of West German ' militarists ' and ' revanchists '.[33]

The initial reactions of the other communist countries were temporizing or even positive. The first Soviet comments on the formation of the new government in Bonn were cautious and non-committal. Acknowledging that a difference in tone could be detected in the pronouncements of the Kiesinger cabinet, the Soviet government organ, *Izvestia*, asserted in December 1966 that if these declarations were to be followed by appropriate deeds, they would hardly go unanswered. The article continued:

The Soviet Union has never believed that the Federal Republic is bewitched by the militarists, that only revanchists live there, that among the West Germans there are no sober-minded, prudent politicians capable of steering the country onto a path of peaceful coexistence with socialist states.[34]

These formulations seem to attest to a certain ambiguity in the Soviet attitude towards West Germany in the sense that, in spite of its scepticism about a sincere change in outlook on the part of the new government, Moscow wished to keep open the option of an improvement of relations with it. Poland too was inclined to reserve judgement. Czechoslovakia and Hungary were also cautious, but they went so far as to receive an official envoy from West Germany in January in order to explore the possibility of establishing diplomatic relations. In contrast to these reactions, the Rumanian response was distinctly positive. Negotiations with West Germany proceeded without great obstacles, and on 31 January 1967 an agreement was reached to exchange ambassadors. The two countries did not allow the question of recognizing East Germany to stand in the way of agreement; each simply stated its position and then they agreed to differ. Mr Ceausescu hailed the step as a major contribution to European security and international *détente* in the spirit of the Bucharest Declaration.[35]

As early as the beginning of January, then, it was clear that if the USSR was to maintain solidarity in its camp it would have to take a more definite stand. Official statements began to harden, and clearly this was not unrelated to the marked nervousness shown by East German leaders at that time.[36] On 13 January 1967 Leonid Brezhnev backed them ostentatiously in a speech at Gorky, in which he described the recognition of the GDR as a precondition for a genuine normalization of the situation in Europe.[37] This was followed up by a dramatic Soviet declaration denouncing the rise of neo-Nazi and militarist forces in West Germany as well as the alleged adherence of the new leadership in Bonn to the revanchist goals of previous West German governments.[38] In a subsequent note to the Federal Republic, the Soviet government stated that the effectiveness of the West German measures against the neo-Nazis would be considered a test of the sincerity of Bonn's efforts to promote security.[39] But since the Soviet government assumed the right to be the sole judge of the effectiveness of these measures, it alone would become the arbitrary judge of the sincerity of West Germany's *Ostpolitik*. All this did not dissuade the Rumanians from bringing their negotiations with West Germany to fruition, but the talks the Hungarians and Czechoslovaks were carrying on with the West German government produced no immediate agreements once the Soviet position had become clear.

A meeting of the foreign ministers of the members of the WTO was held from 8 to 10 February 1967 in Warsaw. Just prior to this, the Polish and Czechoslovak party leadership came out in full support of the tougher line demanded by the East Germans and now strongly endorsed by the Soviet Union.

Mr Gomulka ridiculed the West German thesis—and thereby implicitly the Rumanian position—that the establishment of diplomatic relations with the Federal Republic would promote East–West *détente* and peace in Europe. The main source of tension, according to Mr Gomulka, lay in Bonn: therefore the establishment of diplomatic relations between the Federal Republic and the socialist states would not contribute in any way to an improvement in the political climate of Europe unless there was a concomitant change in the basic West German position relating to the vital interests of the socialist countries.[40] The attitude of the Czechoslovak leadership was indicated by Mr Jiri Hendrych, member of the Presidium of the CPCS, when he stated that it fully supported the declaration of the Soviet government on the dangerous trends in West Germany. He described Bonn's policy as tactical manoeuvring with no change in essence.[41] These indications of support from the Soviet Union, Poland, and Czechoslovakia were cited approvingly by Walter Ulbricht a few days later in a speech in which by implication he criticized the Rumanian stand. He argued that recognition of the existence of two German states in itself did not mean very much. Such recognition acquired a peace-promoting quality only when coupled with a declaration that West Germany renounced its 'revanchist' claim of sole representation.[42]

By the latter half of February 1967, the Soviet leadership was apparently ready to sum up recent trends and to issue an authoritative assessment of the European situation. Repeating almost verbatim the wording of the Bucharest Declaration of July 1966, an article in *Pravda* [43] acknowledged the continued existence of the two main trends in world politics: the peaceful and the aggressive. In the latter group were included forces trying to increase tension and to poison relations among the European states. The main goals of West Germany's *Ostpolitik* were perceived as being (1) to undermine the united front of the socialist countries in their struggle for European security; (2) to isolate the GDR; and (3) to complicate the implementation of the programme adopted by the socialist states at the Bucharest conference.

Moscow was apparently anxious to establish a close link

between American designs in Europe and the new signals coming from Bonn. Thus, having denounced President Johnson's bridge-building efforts as being directed against the commonwealth of socialist countries, the *Pravda* article continued: ' In the distribution of roles under this policy the Kiesinger government has been assigned . . . the task of NATO's authorized agent for disuniting the socialist countries.' The announced willingness of the West German government to establish relations with the East European countries was depicted as the main instrument for these subversive designs. Finally, the article explicitly endorsed Mr Gomulka's thesis that the establishment of diplomatic relations between the Federal Republic and the socialist countries in Eastern Europe would not have any effect in improving the political climate in Europe without a basic shift in West Germany's position. This clearly rebutted the argument of the Rumanian leadership.

The new West German *Ostpolitik* thus had a decidedly unsettling effect on the Soviet camp. The Soviet leaders could not prevent Rumania from establishing diplomatic relations with the Federal Republic, but they were able to check West German courting of their other allies by belittling the importance of diplomatic relations as such and stressing instead the significance of a genuine normalization of West Germany's relations with the East. That would be possible only after West Germany clearly undertook to accept the *status quo* in Central Europe. In spite of the Soviet line, there remained significant discrepancies in Eastern assessments of the European situation. For example, in March 1967 the Hungarian foreign minister, Janos Peter, used the same distinction between the establishment of diplomatic relations and the normalization of relations with West Germany in order to keep open the option of improving relations with Bonn. He implied that an offer to establish diplomatic relations could contribute to normalization if it were sincerely intended to improve conditions.[44] Similarly, Mr Bashev, foreign minister of Bulgaria, stated that West Germany would have to recognize the realities of post-war Europe, but added that he considered this to be a general principle rather than a precondition for an improvement in relations.[45] Only with the adoption of a collective action programme at the Karlovy Vary Conference in April 1967 did a new common platform for the policies of the more conformist members of the socialist camp emerge.

The Karlovy Vary conference

The display of autonomous inclinations—modest though they were in most cases—among the governing élite groups in Eastern Europe gave Moscow reason to speed up the measures to improve the co-ordination and consolidation of the Soviet camp. One of the most significant effects these Soviet efforts had on inter-state relations within the Eastern alliance was the conclusion of several new bilateral treaties between the East European socialist countries in the course of March 1967.[46] The German Democratic Republic, which until then had a bilateral treaty (of 12 June 1964) with the Soviet Union only, was now incorporated in the bilateral treaty system of the East European states.*

At the party level, Moscow attempted to consolidate its own camp by presenting a programme for common action which would be discussed at a conference of the major leaders from all the European communist parties in April 1967 at Karlovy Vary, Czechoslovakia. Prior to that conference (which was preceded by a preparatory meeting in Warsaw, 22–26 February 1967), spokesmen of the CPSU described the prevailing European situation and its requirements in a number of public pronouncements. In a major article in *Pravda* of 10 April 1967 it was stated that ' Europe is going through an important historic period '. ' For the first time ', the article asserted, ' realistic possibilities for ensuring collective security have appeared for the peoples of our continent '. What constituted these realistic possibilities was made clear in an earlier part of the article, which listed the following three factors: (1) the ' insolvency of the policy of strength ' of the Western nations

---

*The GDR concluded a treaty with Poland on 15 Mar. 1967 and with Czecho-slovakia two days later. Similar treaties were concluded with Hungary and Bulgaria on 18 May and 7 Sept. 1967, respectively. The incorporation of the GDR in the East European treaty system was clearly conducive to the general consolidation of the socialist camp sought by the Soviet leadership at that time. Yet the treaty between Poland and the GDR seems also to have been conceived as a reassurance against a possible deal between Moscow and Bonn.

had been revealed; (2) the unwarranted fears of a 'Soviet threat' to Western Europe had been dissipated; and (3) favourable opportunities had opened up for the development of peaceful co-operation among European countries with different social systems.[47]

While the Soviet leadership explicitly acknowledged a general trend in Europe towards peace and international co-operation, it again singled out the West German government as the major culprit on the continent and portrayed its policy as the main stumbling-block on the road to peace and security.[48]

The *policy implications* deduced from this assessment of the European situation were couched in rather militant terms. Mr Brezhnev stressed that it was not sufficient to show willingness to co-operate with those capitalist states in Western Europe that were themselves ready for it; it was also necessary to wage a relentless and uncompromising struggle against all those forces which were attempting to nullify the basic social and political transformation that had taken place during the post-war period in Europe. This in turn led him to emphasize the enormous importance, for future developments, of unanimity and brotherly solidarity among the socialist countries as 'a well tried-out weapon in the struggle against the aggressive forces of imperialism'.[49] Thus, the 'unity of action of the socialist camp' remained the *leitmotiv* in Soviet policy pronouncements on the eve of the conference of communist leaders in Czechoslovakia.

The action programme adopted at Karlovy Vary was clearly designed to create a basis for a broadly conceived communist initiative for peace in Europe. In the view of the main speakers at the conference, a number of propitious circumstances now presented a chance to launch this broad campaign for European security. It seemed to them that there was a general *malaise* in NATO which might possibly result in some members' discontinuing their membership when that option became possible after 1969. The indications in Western Europe of resentment at the massive penetration of American capital there and of criticism of American policy in Vietnam further contributed to the impression that the capitalist countries lacked unity.

Although the Soviet speaker at the conference maintained that these conditions were favourable to joint action by all the ' democratic ' and ' peace-loving ' forces in Europe, he insisted that the effective exploitation of these new opportunities presupposed that ' we ourselves [i.e. the communists] set an example of unity in thought and action '.[50] Thus, it would seem that the Soviet leadership was anxious lest encouragement to co-operate with the ' peace-loving forces ' in Western Europe, including non-communist organizations, were to stimulate the polycentric tendencies among the communist parties. It sought to contain these risks by presenting the exploitation of opportunities opening up in Western Europe not only as an end in itself, but also as an opportunity to strengthen the unity of the world communist movement.

The fact that the Karlovy Vary programme was conceived as a counter-move to West Germany's *détente* offensive in Eastern Europe was indicated by one of its few substantive novelties: the proposal for a treaty by which all European states (including the GDR) would renounce the use or threat of force and interference in internal affairs.[51] In making this treaty proposal, Mr Gomulka emphasized that, ' in contrast to the unilateral declarations or bilateral agreements on the renunciation of force put forward by the German Federal Republic ', the treaty proposed by himself ' would contain concrete pledges on the question of security and the inviolability of the frontiers of all European states '.[52]

In spite of the fact that the Karlovy Vary conference was attended by only the more conformist of the ruling East European communist parties—Rumania and Yugoslavia were not present —the emergence of ' differences of shading in the evaluation of specific events in international life '—to use the language of a *Pravda* article—was inevitable.[53] What, according to the same source, constituted the main element of unity in the fundamental approach of all communist parties participating in the conference was their assessment of the danger to peace arising from West Germany.[54] This consensus on ' the main obstacle ' to peace and security in Europe did not, however, preclude the emergence of significant nuances of opinion, presumably reflecting different priorities and preoccupations.

The positions of the Soviet Union, the GDR, and Poland were very close and virtually represented variations on the same twin themes of ' militarism and revanchism ' emanating from Bonn and ' collusion ' betwen German and American imperialists. A few points are nevertheless worth emphasizing. For one, Mr Brezhnev conveyed the impression that the USSR would be willing to do business with the ' present FRG Government ' provided it adopted a ' sober approach to the present situation in Europe '. For another, he acknowledged that the ' existing trends towards a *détente* on the European Continent ' were ' largely a result of the improvement in bilateral relations between the states of the East and the West '.[55]

No similar confessions were made by either Mr Ulbricht or Mr Gomulka. Speaking of ' two opposing programmes of development and of the role of Germany in Europe ', Mr Gomulka endorsed the East German stand that a lasting peace in Europe ultimately presupposed major transformations of the social system within West Germany.[56] He expressed the view that any government in Bonn representing the interests of the capitalist monopolies would be bound to pursue the same basic foreign policy as its predecessors, aiming in the last resort at the liquidation of the GDR.[57]*

At Karlovy Vary, Walter Ulbricht spoke about such ' symptoms of relaxation ' in Europe as the growing opinion in favour of a non-proliferation treaty and the resistance of certain West European states to American interference in their internal affairs. He did not, however, mention the growth of bilateral contacts between states with different social systems, referred to by Mr Brezhnev, as either cause or effect of a trend towards *détente*. The cold war, according to Mr Ulbricht, was by no means over. Since imperialism had intensified its ' psychological warfare against the socialist countries and our whole movement ', this had become ' the main form of today's

---

*In summer and autumn 1967, the Polish leadership issued statements which could be interpreted as foreshadowing a different approach. Contrary to the position adopted in the spring, Warsaw appeared at least willing to allow the possibility of an accommodation with the ruling group in Bonn. If these new signals indeed indicated an emerging reorientation in Poland's foreign policy, it did not come to fruition in 1968 because of developments in Czechoslovakia.

Cold War '.[58]   The emphasis in Mr Ulbricht's description of prevailing European conditions lay on the link between American and West German imperialism.   The war in Vietnam and the American bridge-building efforts to the East were presented by him as different aspects of one global imperialist strategy against the socialist camp: since a direct confrontation in Europe appeared too risky, the American and West German imperialists were trying to penetrate into the socialist countries by 'economic means and through psychological warfare' and to undermine the socialist system from within.[59]   This was a foretaste of things to come: a year later, under the influence of events in Czechoslovakia, the Central Committee of the CPSU endorsed a very similar view of the international situation.   As yet, however, there was some leeway for less rigid and militant views in the East.

While the Polish and East German leaders conjured up the image of an aggressive West Germany, incorrigible as long as its social system remained unaltered, the Hungarian party leader, Mr Janos Kadar, saw the 'main obstacle' to peace and security in Europe in a different perspective.   He reminded the conference that, following the principle of peaceful co-existence, the socialist countries were striving for 'normal, well-adjusted inter-state relations and mutually beneficial economic ties with all the capitalist countries, including the Federal Republic of Germany'.   He then continued: 'But no headway can be achieved in this field, unless the West German Government genuinely abandons its revenge-seeking ambitions and relinquishes its trumped-up and groundless claim to "exclusive representation".'[60]   According to Mr Kadar, it was the *policy* pursued by the West German government rather than inherent qualities of the ruling circles in Bonn that constituted the main stumbling-block to peace in Europe. Consequently, his interpretation did not in principle exclude the possibility of a change of heart on the part of Bonn even without a major transformation of West German society.   This position did not prevent the Hungarian leader from castigating West German 'monopolists, militarists and revenge-seekers'; nor was there any sign of wavering in his support of the GDR.

But the difference in approach to the problems of European security was unmistakable.*

Due to the composition of the conference at Karlovy Vary the scope for agreement on specific policy measures was naturally limited. The West European communist parties were preoccupied with launching a popular-front type of movement in Western Europe, and, as we have seen, there were latent differences between the representatives of the ruling communist parties in Eastern Europe. The common statement of the participants included a reiteration of those points of the Bucharest Declaration which aimed at safeguarding peace in Europe by consolidating and formalizing the existing *status quo*. This programme was now endorsed not only by the members of the Warsaw Treaty Organization but also by the West European communist parties, which were to bear the main brunt of organizing in their own countries the campaigns for European security planned by the conference. The call to launch these campaigns was specifically directed towards the goal of preventing the ' extension or modification of the Atlantic Treaty '. At the same time, it was linked with a restatement of the proposal to abolish the military organizations of the two alliances put forward at Bucharest.[61] The encouragement to co-operate with all ' democratic ' forces in Europe presumably satisfied the demand of the less dogmatic amongst the European communist parties for a broadly conceived campaign against war and imperialism that would assure them increased freedom of action within the communist movement. But the call for the joint action of all peace-loving forces was also sufficiently oriented towards a ' European Europe ' to give the Soviet Union what it primarily expected: an instrument for the exploitation of anti-American feeling in Western Europe.[62]

It has been noted above [63] that the joint statement issued by the Karlovy Vary conference contained few substantive novelties in comparison with the Bucharest Declaration of 1966. Thus the conspicuous difference between the two programmes for peace in Europe contained in the two documents

---

*A similar stand was taken by the Bulgarian CP; Czechoslovakia's position was more ambiguous.

was largely the result of reformulating previously agreed positions and of eliminating others. The demand for recognition of the Munich agreement of 1938 as invalid from the very outset—merely mentioned in the Bucharest Declaration—was set forth with far greater emphasis at Karlovy Vary, for it was listed as one of the four basic requirements for a European settlement. The enhancement of this point should be seen in the light of the fact that, in the meantime, the new West German government had taken a further step to reassure Czechoslovakia that the Munich treaty was dead and would not be used by Bonn to substantiate any demands. It would seem, therefore, that the prominent place accorded to the point in the Karlovy Vary document may have been due to a wish on the part of the Soviet leadership to restrain those forces in Czechoslovakia which favoured a further *rapprochement* between Prague and Bonn. Among the suggested ' partial measures ' in the field of arms limitations and disarmament, the one about troop withdrawals was now given a distinctly asymmetrical formulation. Instead of the phrase used at Bucharest—' the withdrawal of all troops from territories of other states behind the national frontiers '—the Karlovy Vary conference called for ' the withdrawal of foreign troops from European states ', which clearly applied to American (and Canadian) but not necessarily Soviet forces.

Finally, it is worth noting that the Karlovy Vary programme did not contain any mention of German reunification. Whereas the Bucharest Declaration had spoken of the readiness of the socialist states to carry on their search for a peaceful settlement of the German question and even indicated the path along which this ultimate goal could be reached,[64] there was a conspicuous silence on this issue in the Karlovy Vary statement. At the same time, the claim to a right of ' the peoples ' to concern themselves with ' democracy ' in the Federal Republic was given a far more prominent place in the latter statement. And the implications of the ' consistent defence and development of democracy in the FRG ' were spelt out in great detail.[65] In sum, it amounted to nothing less than a claim to a right of intervention in West German society. Whether this point was introduced in order to consolidate the socialist camp by

F

dramatizing ' the West German threat ' or to prepare a basis for actual interference in West German affairs, or both, is unclear. But the very fact that it could be conceived in either way illustrates the difficulty of conclusively establishing the nature of communist designs in Europe.

What appears to be less open to question is the fact that in the wake of Bonn's active efforts to improve relations with the East, the German issue had become extremely sensitive for Moscow, Warsaw, and East Berlin. Collectively, it could be approached by the socialist states only in terms that repeated standard demands for a consolidation of the existing *status quo* in Central Europe and encouraged all communists to greater watchfulness to counter the allegedly rising danger from aggressive forces in the Federal Republic.

Long-term goals and preferences

The analysis of declarations and speeches made in connection with the two communist conferences in 1966 and 1967 has brought to light some of the differences in priorities and approach between Moscow and individual East European governments. Yet, it is clear that the strong pressures to conform which characterize gatherings of this sort usually set strict limits on the formulation of positions reflecting divergences of view. These pressures are less noticeable in declarations about long-term goals not immediately related to impending policy decisions. A scrutiny of this type of official pronouncement may help us to distinguish more clearly the preferences of different Eastern governments with regard to the future of East–West relations.

The Soviet design for Europe

The traditional Soviet formula for a peaceful order in Europe has been the establishment of an all-European system of collective security. During 1954–5, Moscow was at pains to expound this idea in considerable detail with a view to preventing the consolidation of NATO and particularly the rearmament and full integration of West Germany in the Western alliance. This policy failed when the Federal Republic entered NATO in 1955 and subsequently became rearmed.

The Soviet Union retaliated by establishing the WTO, and after an abortive attempt to transform the two military alliances and replace them with a European security pact, Moscow's interest in alternative security arrangements slackened off.[66]

In the *détente* atmosphere of the mid-1960s, the idea of a European security system was warmed up again. This time, however, the Soviet leadership avoided putting forward a concrete plan for the restructuring of security arrangements in Europe. Two main ideas nevertheless stood out as basic elements in most Soviet statements related to a European settlement during this latter period: (1) the need to safeguard ' socialist achievements ' in Europe; and (2) the insistence on a purely ' European ' framework for a future peaceful order.[67] It would be incorrect to assume that these two elements in Moscow's concept reflected a dichotomy between ' defensive ' and ' offensive ' aspirations. Both elements were very probably motivated by ' defensive ' concerns. But they were related to different aspects of Soviet policy in Europe, one being focused on keeping a firm hold on that part of the continent which ever since 1945 had been under Soviet control, the other on increasing Soviet leverage in the other part of Europe. Both these concerns were clearly reflected in the position which the Soviet Union adopted on the German question in the 1960s. Whenever the Soviet leaders felt inclined to espouse the aim of a ' peaceful solution of the German problem ', they demanded not only that discussions of the issue must start by recognizing the territorial *status quo* in Central Europe but also that a future settlement must ensure the ' social achievements ' of the German Democratic Republic. To the extent that they showed any interest in promoting a process of peaceful change in Europe, they envisaged a development leading to ' peaceful ' and ' democratic ' conditions in *both* parts of Germany. Since according to Soviet contentions the situation in the GDR fully met these requirements, this position might be interpreted as a demand for the transformation of West German society rather than an indication of willingness to accept changes in both parts of Germany. However, the Soviet stand on relations with West Germany was always left sufficiently ambiguous not to foreclose the option of a future deal with a non-communist government in Bonn.

The practical steps which the Soviet leadership suggested for attaining its preferred European constellation included measures of ' *military détente* ' (as defined in earlier Soviet or East European proposals, such as the denuclearization of Central Europe) and ' the development of peaceful, mutually advantageous ties among all European states '.[68]

In the wake of the progressing European *détente* of 1966–7, it became increasingly difficult for the Soviet leadership to promote pan-European co-operation without at the same time jeopardizing the consolidation of its power position in Central and Eastern Europe. This induced Moscow to soft-pedal pan-European co-operative ventures, unless they could be formulated in distinctly anti-American terms. At Karlovy Vary, for example, Mr Brezhnev praised the trend towards ' co-operation in the economy, science, technology, and culture both on a bilateral and an all-European scale ' but ascribed this tendency to an alleged ' growing desire to strengthen national independence and get rid of the dictation of the dollar '.[69]

Preferences and preoccupations of other East European states

Amongst the East European leaders, those in the German Democratic Republic came closest to sharing the ideas of the Soviet leadership with regard to a future European settlement. Thus the GDR was the only East European state which expressly accepted the Soviet concept of a peaceful Europe from which the influence of the United States had been eliminated militarily, politically, and economically to the greatest possible extent. Typically, an East German analysis published in 1968 spoke of ' socialist Europe ' as constituting two-thirds of the continent, while the remaining *Resteuropa* was said to be under the rule of ' the imperialist world power, the United States of America '.[70] In the opinion of the East German leaders, the only conceivable framework for a European settlement was therefore one that combined the consolidation of ' socialist achievements ' in Eastern and Central

Europe with maximum leverage to achieve 'democratic transformation' in West Europe, or at least in West Germany.[71]

The positions adopted by the other Soviet allies in Eastern Europe with regard to the shape of a peaceful order in Europe were more ambiguous. They represented a spectrum of attitudes, ranging from cautious Czechoslovak and Polish hints that a durable peace presupposed some kind of American participation, to the contention, implicitly conveyed in Rumanian declarations,[72] that European security would be best safeguarded if the influence of *both* superpowers were kept within distinct limits. The problem of formulating a common goal that would encompass these divergent attitudes was usually solved by resorting to the ill-defined concept of an all-European collective security system.* The nuances in approach that nevertheless existed can be inferred from an analysis of the specific steps suggested by individual East European governments in order to promote 'European security'.

They advocated three types of measures as being conducive to a stable peace in Europe: (1) the recognition of the present *status quo* by the Western powers, and by the Federal Republic in particular; (2) the limitation and regulation of armaments in Central Europe; and (3) the development of East–West co-operation in Europe. Although all East European governments favoured these measures, each type had its special supporters. East Germany and Poland were especially anxious to emphasize the importance and implications of recognizing the *status quo*. Poland was also most active in proposing different plans for the limitation of armaments in Central Europe, while Rumania and Hungary, as well as Czechoslovakia under Mr Dubcek, were the most articulate advocates of promoting co-operation between East and West.

If the consolidation of 'socialist achievements' in Eastern Europe was a primary consideration for Moscow, it was a

---

*Rumania, though a signatory of the Bucharest Declaration of 1966, which recommended ' the formation in Europe of a system of collective security ', and very much in favour of dismantling military alliances, never itself proposed that these should be replaced by a new security system. Instead, Mr Ceausescu suggested the development of co-operative ties among all European states based on mutual confidence and respect, non-intervention in internal affairs, and complete equality.

life-and-death issue for the rulers of the GDR. The recognition of the East German state by the West was therefore presented by them as *the* central question of European security.[73]

It is worth noting that in 1964 the Polish leadership considered recognition of the territorial and political *status quo* by the Federal Republic to be *the starting point* in a process eventually leading to German reunification.[74] In the spring of 1966, Warsaw still upheld this linkage by demanding ' the recognition of the existence of the German Democratic Republic as an equal German state and *a partner for the unification of Germany* '.[75] After 1967, however, the link between these two elements in the Polish concept became tenuous at best. Instead the emphasis was put more than ever on ' the existence, development, and stabilization ' of the GDR as ' a precondition for peace and security in Europe '.[76]

Ever since the late 1950s the Polish government had favoured schemes for arms limitations in Central Europe. The Polish proposals to that effect—from the original Rapacki plan to the modified version of the Gomulka plan—could serve several purposes related to Poland's national interests. In as far as these plans envisaged the consolidation of the military and political *status quo* in Central Europe, they were in line with the main thrust of Soviet policy. At the same time, they were also conceived as *détente* measures since the limitation of armaments in the proposed sensitive region would, it was argued, bring about a relaxation of tension and thus be conducive to East–West *rapprochement*.[77] Finally, the Polish initiatives in this field served as a focus for Poland's active diplomacy and as an opportunity for Warsaw to exploit its marginal freedom of action.[78]

While none of the other East European states displayed similar activity, official Hungarian views and suggestions in the field of arms regulations are worth mentioning because they were rather close, at least conceptually, to some of the arms control notions prevailing in the West. Hungary seemed to attribute special importance to establishing relations between NATO and the Warsaw Treaty Organization in such a way as to minimize the risk of the outbreak of war. The Hungarian proposals to that effect, which in the West would be labelled measures in inter-bloc arms control and crisis management, were considered to be fully compatible with the ultimate aim of eliminating the military alliances in Europe.[79]

Hungary and Rumania were the main champions of East–West co-operation in Europe as a means to a peaceful order. Rumania put special emphasis on the development of *bilateral* relations and argued that ' life itself ' required ' the liquidation of artificial barriers . . . which have hitherto prevented the free flow of material assets and ideas '. The replacement of the blocs by ' a climate of co-operation between all countries of our continent ' was therefore labelled by the Rumanian deputy foreign minister, Mr Malitza, an essential condition for the solution of the major problems of peace and security.[80] Hungary, on the other hand, favoured the development of *regional* co-operation in different parts of Europe as a preliminary to pan-European security arrangements. The Hungarian government especially cherished the idea of co-operation across political and ideological barriers in the Danube valley, and in 1967, the Hungarian parliament proposed a pan-European treaty of security and co-operation, the conclusion of which, it was hoped, would be facilitated by regional agreements.[81]

Some conclusions

Analysis of the official pronouncements of communist governments during the period 1966–7 reveals that they were pursuing two main goals: (1) the development of mutually advantageous co-operation between East and West within an ' all-European ' context; and (2) the attainment of a new system of European security. The first objective was seen both as an end in itself—more by the Rumanians and Hungarians than by some of their allies—and as a stepping-stone on the road to the second goal. The policy requirements that followed from these goals, which were agreed upon at Bucharest and Karlovy Vary at least in broad terms, were by necessity very different in character. The first essentially called for an extension of contacts between Eastern and Western Europe and put a premium on experimenting with co-operative schemes between institutions, enterprises, and individuals

belonging to different social systems.   The goal of a ' collective
security system ', which in the last analysis meant nothing
less than a European settlement *à la Russe*, primarily required
forceful spade-work in Western Europe, usually labelled the
' struggle for European security '.   What made these policy
requirements at least temporarily compatible was not only the
fact that the development of pan-European co-operation was
explicitly endorsed by Moscow as a means serving the ultimate
goal of ' European security '.   In addition, the concept of
' obstacles ' to pan-European security and co-operation which
the Soviet Union employed enabled Moscow to advocate
concentrating efforts to eliminate these hindrances—primarily
the forces of ' militarism and revanchism ' in West Germany
—and yet maintain that this was a contribution to improving
collaboration between East and West.

In the course of 1967, the inherent tension between the two
approaches to European security and co-operation became
very acute as Soviet pronouncements on the subject acquired
an increasingly militant note.   This in turn appears to have
been due largely to the fact that by the end of 1967 the ' struggle
for European security ' was seen from Moscow in a different
perspective from that of only eighteen months or two years
earlier.

The evidence seems to suggest that in 1966 the Soviet
leadership stepped up the campaign for ' European security '
in the belief that the prospect of achieving a new constellation
of forces in Europe by 1969 was sufficiently promising to make
the effort worthwhile.   Moscow was apparently willing to add
at least marginally to the fluidity of the European situation by
hinting at the possibility of alternative security arrangements
in Europe and by sanctioning collaboration between communists and other ' progressive ' forces in Western Europe.
During 1967, however, the slogan of ' European security ' was
used by Soviet spokesmen primarily in connection with efforts
to hedge against the destabilizing effect of West Germany's
détente offensive in Eastern Europe.   In Soviet declaratory
policy the ' struggle for European security ' thus became closely
linked with Moscow's concern about the consolidation of its
own sphere of influence in Europe—rather than with the

exploitation of opportunities opening up in Western Europe. This, in turn, made it more difficult to present the ' struggle for European security ' as an element in a strategy aiming at the establishment of a system of mutually advantageous co-operation within a pan-European framework. The requirements posed by the objective of developing ' business-like ' contacts and co-operation with the capitalist countries were hardly compatible with increasingly stringent demands for a relentless struggle against Western imperialists, revanchists, and militarists. While the priority of consolidating Soviet influence in Eastern Europe was probably never seriously questioned within the decision-making body in the Kremlin, the wish to uphold the *détente* image in the West and at the same time to stabilize conditions in Eastern Europe confronted Moscow with a genuine dilemma. This was sharply accentuated by developments within Czechoslovakia during 1968 and the concomitant trend towards further fragmentation of the socialist camp, for what these events seemed to jeopardize was not only the predominance of the Soviet Union in Eastern Europe—a major stake indeed—but ultimately the power position of the ruling communist élite in the Soviet Union itself as well.

THE INVASION OF CZECHOSLOVAKIA, 1968: REPERCUSSIONS IN EAST AND WEST

THE central issue in the controversy that developed during 1968 between the new Czechoslovak leadership under Alexander Dubcek and the Brezhnev–Kosygin regime in Moscow was about the role of the communist party in a socialist society. According to the Action Programme adopted by the Central Committee of the Czechoslovak communist party on 5 April 1968, the party was not to implement its leading role ' by ruling over the society but by serving its free, progressive socialist development most faithfully '. Thus, the party could not ' force its line by orders, but by the works of its members and the veracity of its ideals '.[1] These guide-lines, which clearly foreshadowed a new model of socialist society, must have been completely unacceptable to communist leaders for whom authoritarian rule and central control by a party élite remained the main principles of government.

Differences on such basic issues could not leave foreign policy questions unaffected. It was therefore natural that Europe and the world at large began to look distinctly different as seen from official quarters in Moscow and Prague. The unfolding Czechoslovak drama in turn influenced assessments of the European situation in most countries in the East and the West. The nature and implication of these shifts in perspective will be analysed in the following chapter. It does not claim to be an account of events in Czechoslovakia during that dramatic year but is rather a review of authoritative statements which show how various governments perceived the impact of the crisis on East–West relations in Europe. The analysis of the period prior to the invasion has been focused on the divergence between Czechoslovak and Soviet views. The emphasis of the chapter as a whole, however, is on the immediate aftermath of the invasion and the modification of long-range perspectives by East and West alike.

The divergence between Czechoslovak and Soviet foreign policy statements before 21 August 1968

The general hardening of Moscow's policy, noticeable in 1967, became even more marked during 1968. This could be seen in the more rigid and defensive policies the Soviet government adopted on domestic as well as international issues.[2] With regard to East–West relations in Europe, official Soviet attitudes were more than ever characterized by emphatic warnings about the machinations of imperialists in general and West German militarists and revanchists in particular. In the context of the Soviet–Czechoslovak controversy, the inflation of these threat perceptions played a crucial role. Now as earlier the spectre of West German aggressiveness served as the main instrument to counteract West Germany's influence in Eastern Europe, which, in spite of the success the Soviet leaders had had in containing it in 1967, apparently continued to worry them.

For the new leaders in Prague, on the other hand, the development of economic relations with the West, and especially with West Germany, was an indispensable component of the programme designed to revitalize Czechoslovakia's economy. This in itself would cause Czechoslovak officials to hesitate about emphasizing a threat from any of the Western powers, but in addition they became caught up in the dynamics of free speech and information and were virtually forced to phrase their foreign policy declarations in a manner distinctly different from Moscow's.[3] Thus the divergences in official views regarding East–West relations became a conspicuous feature of the controversy between Moscow and Prague.

At the plenary sessions of the Central Committee of the CPCS in December 1967 and January 1968, the winds of political fortune were blowing against the regime of Mr Novotny who had lost support by his policy of least possible change. Even after the appointment of Alexander Dubcek as First Secretary of the Central Committee, however, it took several months before new ideas were more generally accepted and their implementation could begin in earnest. One of the most significant steps in the unfolding process of democratization was the lifting of censorship, which in turn decisively added to the momentum of the whole process of transformation in Czechoslovakia. The greater assertiveness and self-assurance characterizing official Czechoslovak pronouncements during the spring of 1968 should thus be seen against the background of emerging signs of popular response and support, cautious at first but more and more emphatic as the vitalizing spirit of free speech began to pervade the Czechoslovak body politic. The development can be observed in all fields of political and social life, including foreign affairs.

The early declarations of the new leadership essentially repeated the standard positions on the major foreign policy issues.[4] During March 1968, however, the open debates on all aspects of politics in Czechoslovakia began to influence official pronouncements on international problems. By the end of the month, relations between Prague and East Berlin had become very strained due to repeated East German criticism of developments in Czechoslovakia. The official organ of the Czechoslovak party, *Rude Pravo*, proposed then that Czechoslovakia should embark upon an independent course in its relations with West Germany. Instead of following the East German lead, the paper argued, Prague might attempt to influence developments in West Germany in order to normalize relations between the two countries.[5]

These new ideas were formulated far more cautiously when Alexander Dubcek addressed a plenary session of the Central Committee of the CPCS on 1 April 1968.[6] Yet even from that speech it could clearly be inferred that the change of leadership in Prague would have tangible repercussions in the field of foreign affairs. To be sure, Mr Dubcek asserted that ' just as the socialist nature of our further path is inviolable, so are the basic principles of Czechoslovakia's foreign policy orientation.' But in his description of the new tasks for Czechoslovakia in international affairs there were new nuances, as when he called for a more effective European policy, which would foster the strengthening of peaceful relations in Europe and the development of co-operation between countries with different social systems, and when he declared that Czechoslovakia was

' interested above all in a peaceful settlement of the German question '.*

The Action Programme adopted by the Central Committee a few days later corroborated these new signals of change. The most dramatically innovative elements in it were the proposals dealing with the revitalization of the economy, the change in the decision-making procedures, and the new role of the party in the continued transformation of Czechoslovak society. Clearly the foreign policy section of the Action Programme was intended to promote more effective participation by Czecho-slovakia in the international division of labour and to expose its economy to the competitive climate of the world market —two basic goals set out in the economic section of the Programme. With regard to future relations with Czechoslo-vakia's neighbours, the wording of the Programme was very evenly balanced. It reasserted the determination of the new Czechoslovak leadership to adhere to the alliance with the Soviet Union and the other socialist countries as a basic and unalterable principle of Czechoslovak foreign policy. At the same time, the Programme emphasized that the needs and opportunities of Czechoslovakia as an industrialized country in the heart of Europe required it to play a more active role in European politics and to develop mutually advantageous relations with all states and international organizations. The usual tribute was paid to the German Democratic Republic, ' the first socialist state on German soil ' which constituted ' an essential factor of peace in Europe '. As to the Federal Repub-lic, however, the Action Programme mentioned not only revanchist tendencies but also ' realistic forces ' there, a phrase which at the time had virtually disappeared from the Soviet vocabulary.[7]

On none of the major substantive issues related to European

---

*It is probably symptomatic that Dubcek referred to the ' peaceful settlement of the German question ' as having ' cardinal importance for European security ' —almost exactly Brezhnev's words to the 23rd Party Congress of the CPSU in Mar. 1966. Since then, however, the Soviet position had hardened, and, as indicated in ch. 2, settlement of the German question had not been mentioned in the Karlovy Vary programme. Thus, when Dubcek referred to the German issue in these terms, it signified a cautious, yet visible, manifestation of an inde-pendent stand by the new leaders in Prague.

security had the new leadership in Prague taken a position which differed from those included in the collective programme of the European communist parties adopted at Karlovy Vary in 1967, yet the difference in perspective and emphasis was unmistakable. Instead of militant exhortation to ' struggle for European security ', a phrase with distinct anti-imperialist and anti-West German overtones, the pronouncements of the new leadership in Prague conveyed the impression that they were primarily concerned with developing peaceful co-operation across ideological borderlines.[8]

It is against this divergence in outlook that the adamant position of the Soviet leadership, reflected in a number of pronouncements in March and April 1968, should be seen. While they revealed the Soviet leaders' general concern that imperialist ideology had taken the offensive, and while the admonitions contained in them were mainly directed to the Soviet people, these declarations also served as a kind of general parameter for Soviet declaratory policy during the unfolding controversy with Prague.

On 10 April 1968 the Soviet leadership summed up its views of the international situation in a resolution adopted at the plenary session of the CPSU Central Committee. It confirmed ' the correctness of the policy of exposing revanchism and militarism in West Germany ' and called for increased solidarity of the socialist countries and all anti-imperialist forces in the struggle against West German imperialism. The plenary session also noted ' that the present state of historical developments is characterized by sharp exacerbation of the ideological struggle between capitalism and socialism '. Repeating similar previous pronouncements by Leonid Brezhnev and other leaders,[9] the Central Committee gave warning that ' the entire huge apparatus of anti-communist propaganda ' was now attempting to weaken the unity of socialist countries and ' undermine socialist society from within '. The primary task confronting the Soviet Union was therefore said to be ' implacable struggle against enemy ideology, resolute exposure of the schemes of imperialism, communist upbringing of CPSU members and all the working people, and intensification of all the Party's ideological activities '.[10]

Thus, the Soviet leaders on the one hand conjured up the image of a massive attempt on the part of the class enemies and their supporters to undermine individual socialist countries as well as the cohesion of the whole socialist camp. On the other hand, they depicted the ideological front as ' the sharpest front of the class struggle '.[11] This double approach was henceforth consistently used to denounce developments in Czechoslovakia as evidence of ' counter-revolutionary ' machinations, directed against the true interests of the Czechoslovak people and the whole socialist camp.

The intensification of pressures against Czechoslovakia by the Soviet Union and her ' faithful ' East European allies that followed upon the publication on 27 June 1968 of the open letter entitled ' Two Thousand Words ' [12] by the Czech author, Ludvik Vaculik, was accompanied by a rupture in the confidential dialogue between Moscow and Bonn that had been going on since early 1967. This, it would seem, was a logical step for the Soviet leadership to take in the given circumstances. The credibility of Soviet warnings of a threat from West Germany, echoed in Warsaw and East Berlin, was not easy to uphold against contradictory evidence available to growing numbers of East Europeans. The very fact that secret Soviet–West German diplomatic exchanges were taking place on a subject immediately related to the Central European issues—renunciation of force agreements—must have made significantly more difficult the task of those who were trying to propagate the image of a West Germany dominated by revanchists and militarists. In view of the almost automatic Soviet recourse to ' the German threat ' as an instrument of consolidation in Eastern Europe and the marked exacerbation of the Soviet–Czechoslovak conflict, Moscow was apparently now induced to discontinue the talks with Bonn and thus to adopt a more consistently hostile posture towards the Federal Republic.[13]

The divergence in the attitude of Moscow and Prague regarding West Germany continued, however, until the very eve of the invasion. Thus the so-called ' Warsaw letter ' of 15 July 1968, signed by the leaders of the five powers that less than six weeks later were to send troops into Czechoslovakia, denounced the West German government as invariably pursuing a course hostile to the interests of the socialist countries.[14] The Czechoslovak reply, on the other hand, carefully avoided any vilifying comments about the government in Bonn.[15]

The meeting between representatives of the five ' fraternal ' parties and the Czechoslovak party leadership in Bratislava on 3 August 1968 produced a joint statement which included an appraisal of the international situation and European developments. The latter contained many militant phrases, directed specifically against West Germany. Yet it also included a general declaration of support to all forces that ' fight against militarism and revanchism and for democratic progress ', a clause which seems to have been added at the request of the Czechoslovak leaders.[16] Thus, each side had been able to insert phrases that would enable it to interpret any situation according to its own preferences. This was clearly borne out by subsequent developments.

On 16 August 1968 a new Czechoslovak–Rumanian treaty of friendship and co-operation was signed. It not only limited the purpose of the Warsaw Treaty Organization to defence against NATO but also conspicuously lacked any explicit reference to ' the West German threat '. To be sure, both the preamble and Article 7 of the treaty alluded to the potential threat emanating from imperialist, militarist, and revanchist forces, but nowhere in the document was there a suggestion of an *imminent* danger, nowhere was a direct link established between this *potential* threat and current tendencies in the Federal Republic.[17] This was very much at variance with the views prevailing in Moscow. A few days later, Czechoslovakia was occupied. And the Soviet leadership could argue that it was necessary to render ' fraternal internationalist support ' to the Czechoslovak people in order to protect them against a threat which their leaders were patently unable or unwilling to acknowledge appropriately.

This is not to suggest that the divergence in official views described above was in itself necessarily a decisive factor in bringing about Moscow's decision to intervene. Indeed the official Soviet comments on the results of the meetings in Cierna and Bratislava indicated Moscow's primary concern with ideological infection.[18] The Czechoslovak experiments in humanistic socialism were clearly viewed as ultimately threatening the power base of the Soviet élite at home. Nevertheless, the foreign policy issues were a recurring theme in the polemics accompanying the events that culminated so tragically on 21 August 1968, for the whole drama turned around a closely interconnected complex of domestic and international, ideological and strategic issues.

The impact of the invasion of Czechoslovakia on East–West relations in Europe

The invasion of Czechoslovakia took the West by surprise and officials indicated publicly for the first time that the Soviet concept of *détente* was quite different from theirs after all. In the period of uncertainty that followed, the countries in both East and West reacted by conferring more intensely with their allies and by reassessing their basic assumptions about the future of East–West relations.

Some Western assumptions

It was natural that developments in Czechoslovakia during the spring of 1968 aroused popular interest and expectations in the West. The determined efforts of the new leadership in Prague to safeguard basic human rights in a socialist society and to develop a novel blueprint for ' socialist construction ', together with the new encouragement given by Prague to the idea of co-operation across ideological boundaries, were all apt to elicit Western approval, not to say enthusiasm. Governmental attitudes in the West were to a large extent shaped by these spontaneous public reactions.[19]

Reflecting on official American attitudes towards developments in Czechoslovakia prior to the invasion, Under Secretary of State Katzenbach stated on 16 October 1968 that Washington looked upon internal change within the Soviet bloc as an important part of the process of *détente*. We believed that, as Eastern European governments were able to relax controls and break with the unreasoning attitudes of the past the prospects for cooperation to reach an acceptable accommodation in Europe would be enhanced.[20]

G

This assessment was corroborated by pronouncements made before the invasion by American officials including Mr Katzenbach himself.[21] In the Federal Republic as well, two public speeches delivered by Willy Brandt in June 1968 seemed to indicate that he was inclined to describe the developments in the Soviet alliance as roughly parallel to similar tendencies to fragmentation in the Western camp.[22]

Thus Western officials gave no indication that they were aware of the extent to which developments in Czechoslovakia constituted a fundamental challenge for the Soviet leadership. This may partly have been due to observing inter-state relations in the East through the ' glasses ' of their own experiences in the West. Moreover, the Soviet Union attempted to convey to the West a general image of peaceful intent and reasonableness, which tended to conceal Moscow's concern to hedge against the repercussions of the European *détente* within its own camp. As a result, because of the Western inclination to assume a greater symmetry in intra-bloc relations in East and West than existed, Western officials attributed to the Soviet leadership less determination to quash the Czechoslovak reforms, by force if necessary, than subsequent events disclosed.

Some immediate policy conclusions

In one respect both East and West arrived at similar conclusions about what action was necessary immediately following the invasion: both sides emphasized the need for close cooperation *within* their respective alliances. In the case of the Soviet Union the call for a further strengthening of cohesion within the socialist camp was part and parcel of a campaign to justify the invasion itself. For that purpose the Soviet government further dramatized the ' German threat ' during the weeks immediately following the invasion. The Soviet action was thus construed as ' a decisive blow to the aggressive plans of the imperialist forces ' and even as a step protecting ' the peoples of Europe from the threat of a new military conflagration '.[23] Furthermore, in an attempt to make the threat more credible Moscow introduced the concept of ' peaceful counter-revolution ', allegedly a new, highly insidious tactic of the imperialists to mislead gullible people by citing the necessity of 'improving' socialism.[24] These conclusions were supported by authoritative Polish pronouncements and, most emphatically, by the East German leaders.[25]

In the West the need for greater cohesion and co-operation within NATO was probably most spontaneously expressed in Bonn where the threat from the dramatic events in Eastern Europe was felt with greater immediacy.[26] But the distinctly perceptible trend towards a *rapprochement* between Washington and Paris in the autumn of 1968 added to the general notion pervading the official circles of Western capitals that it was not only desirable but also possible to achieve a revitalization of the Western alliance.[27]

These trends in official Western opinion were clearly related to what was seen as an increased threat to common Western interests and values. This threat was mainly attributed to greater uncertainty about Moscow's *intentions* and the concomitant difficulty of predicting Soviet behaviour.[28] This was of special significance in view of the fact that the assessment of Soviet intentions had been adopted by NATO as a criterion for Western military preparedness. In the opinion of the American secretary of defense, Clark Clifford, the occupation of Czechoslovakia did not alter the military *capabilities* of the WTO, except that strong Soviet forces, kept in a very high state of alert, were now stationed closer to the West German border, thus constituting a more direct threat to West Germany.[29] Most Western military observers agreed that this in itself did not fundamentally change the over-all strategic situation between East and West in Europe. Some politicians in the West favoured greater alliance cohesion on more general grounds. They argued that the invasion had stopped the process of fragmentation within the Warsaw Pact, at least for the time being; hence, it was felt, the Western powers ought to make a determined effort to check the erosion within their own ranks.[30]

Corresponding to this parallel reaction in East and West to strengthen alliance cohesion, there was a certain similarity in the other main conclusion both sides seemed to draw from the whole Czechoslovak affair, namely that it was necessary to prevent another crisis of the same kind from occurring. It was probably at least partly with this in view that the Soviet

leadership issued a declaration of basic principles pertaining
to the relations between socialist countries. Although the
central idea in the concept had been expressed by authoritative
Soviet spokesmen previously, it was formulated more coher-
ently and with greater emphasis than before in a policy-making
article in *Pravda* on 26 September and in an address by foreign
minister Andrei Gromyko before the United Nations General
Assembly on 3 October 1968.[31] The central tenet of the new
doctrine was the contention that ' laws and legal standards '
are ' subject to the laws of class struggle '. This implied that
the concept of *sovereignty* in the general sense of ' state sovereignty ' had to be subordinated to the interests of the socialist
community as a whole. In the words of the *Pravda* article,

> The sovereignty of each socialist country cannot be set up in
> opposition to the interests of the socialist world and the interests of
> the world revolutionary movement. Lenin demanded that all
> communists ' fight against small-nation narrow-mindedness, seclu-
> sion and isolation, consider the whole and the general, subordinate
> the particular to the general interest '.[32]

The author of this article, Mr S. Kovalev, was indeed on safe
ideological ground when he claimed that the theory of limited
sovereignty was in full accordance with Lenin's views.[33] The
Soviet leadership, however, had earlier found it inopportune
to propagate this thesis with full clarity. In the autumn of
1968 Moscow nevertheless decided to do so, in response to
severe world-wide criticism of the invasion of Czechoslovakia.
It seems then, that the main purpose of the new theory, which
became known as the ' Brezhnev doctrine ', was to justify
acts perpetrated against a socialist country.[34] Once stated,
however, it became a precedent on the basis of which future
decisions to intervene could be taken. Thus the doctrine could
perform a useful function by dissuading leaders and élite groups
within the Warsaw Treaty area from introducing reforms or
experiments of the Czechoslovak type. In view of the vague-
ness of the concept ' socialist community ' the new doctrine
could also be used to intimidate the Yugoslav leaders and thus
to dissuade them from further ' meddling ' in Eastern Europe.
If the invasion of Czechoslovakia called for some Western
reaction to deter Moscow from using force in the future, the

Brezhnev doctrine, with its possible implication of Soviet designs on the so-called 'grey areas' in Europe, seemed to make a response from the West so much more urgent.

A warning to Moscow was drawn up and discussed at NATO's ministerial meeting in mid-November 1968. In the version finally adopted it read:

The members of the Alliance urge the Soviet Union in the interests of world peace, to refrain from using force and interfering in the affairs of other states. Determined to safeguard the freedom and independence of their countries, they could not remain indifferent to any development which endangers their security. Clearly any Soviet intervention directly or indirectly affecting the situation in Europe or in the Mediterranean would create an international crisis with grave consequences.[35]

No countries were mentioned in the text of the *communiqué*, for to have done so might have created difficulties. Besides, unless all countries in potential danger were named (and there was nowhere near unanimity amongst the allies for extending NATO's commitments thus far), Moscow might infer that it had *carte blanche* from NATO to act in unnamed countries. The wording finally adopted gave by its imprecision some degree of deterrence.

In the closed ministerial meeting, the possible consequences of further hypothetical Soviet moves were discussed, and special attention appears to have been paid to the position of Rumania and Yugoslavia. On balance, the Brussels meeting left the impression that NATO was considering giving some sort of protection to countries outside its membership, although it was unclear which countries might be potential recipients and in what way they might be aided.[36]

As far as immediate policy consequences were concerned, then, the main effect of the Czechoslovak crisis was to accentuate the need for cohesion within the two military alliances. A secondary effect was an ambiguous extension of the spheres of influence of the two superpowers, at least in terms of 'declaratory' as distinct from military postures. Indeed, it could be argued that NATO and the WTO had begun to overlap.

Repercussions on long-range prospects for peace in Europe

Even though the Czechoslovak crisis was unquestionably a critical experience for both East and West, it did not lead to a revision of the declared foreign policy goals of any major power in Europe. During the crisis, both before and after the invasion, the Soviet Union insisted on the necessity of strengthening the Warsaw Treaty Organization as an immediate requirement, yet it formally reaffirmed its commitment to the *long-term* programme for European security adopted at the Bucharest conference in 1966, which included the proposal for the elimination of military alliances in Europe.[37]

In the West, President Johnson reaffirmed the goals of United States policy concerning East–West relations in Europe in one of his early speeches after the invasion of Czechoslovakia by referring to his 1966 proposals, which were intended to bring about ' a coming together of Germany and a healing of the deep wounds across the entire face of Europe '.[38] Even the government of the Federal Republic—the Western country perhaps most immediately affected by the Czechoslovak crisis—reconfirmed the long-term goals of its policy towards the East shortly after the invasion.[39] Similar views were later expressed by the NATO parliamentarians at the annual meeting of the North Atlantic Assembly in mid-November 1968. The resolutions adopted by the Assembly included an explicit endorsement of the concept coined by the West German leaders of a ' durable European peace order ' as the only conceivable context for the solution of the German question.[40]

If the declared long-term goals of the major powers in Europe remained largely unchanged by the crisis, there was ample evidence that the governments concerned had begun to reassess the *means* by which these goals could be attained. In the West, the repercussions were more noticeable in the policy declarations of the two main continental states, France and West Germany, than in those of the Anglo-Saxon powers. The reason for this would seem to be that while programmes for East–West reconciliation in Europe constituted major elements in French and West German foreign policy, American and British ideas—they can scarcely be called programmes—

were neither explicitly formulated nor forcefully promoted. For Paris and Bonn the invasion of Czechoslovakia therefore meant a major set-back in their foreign policy, calling for a fundamental reappraisal of earlier assumptions.

We have previously noted that prior to the invasion American and British leaders had viewed a balanced reduction of forces in Central Europe as the single most favoured step to further the relaxation of tension in Europe. Progress in that field, they hoped, would improve the international climate significantly and ultimately open up possibilities for a European settlement.[41] This road became blocked for the time being by the occupation of Czechoslovakia, but again there was some similarity in the approach the United States and Great Britain adopted, for both seemed to emphasize the need for making progress in the unification of Western Europe. The incentive for Washington to adopt this line was the prospect that a more unified Western Europe could play a greater role in NATO. Even though that might not reduce the risks of the confrontation in Europe, it could at least lessen the cost to the American taxpayer. For Britain, greater West European unity as a means to a more stable Europe gave the government an opportunity to stress how its Europe-oriented policy was to the common advantage of Britain and continental Europe. Typically, Britain's secretary of state for defence, Mr Denis Healey, argued in favour of creating a ' sense of European identity ' within the Western alliance and suggested that this might not only give the Europeans greater leverage on Washington but that in the long run it might also promote a European settlement.[42]

The occupation of Czechoslovakia clearly demonstrated that at least two of the major preconditions for a stable peace in Europe envisaged by President de Gaulle would not be fulfilled in the foreseeable future, namely the evolution of Soviet methods of government away from ' totalitarian restraint imposed on its land and on others ', and the emergence of the nations between Bug and Elbe as independent actors ' able to play their role in a renewed Europe '.[43] The dramatic events in Czechoslovakia revealed a basic dilemma in French policy towards the East in the 1960s. President de Gaulle had

attempted to encourage the national self-assertion and independence of the smaller East European states and yet at the
same time to cultivate and develop close co-operation with
Moscow.   In the late summer of 1968 it became clear that
these two lines of policy were, to say the least, very difficult to
combine.   In the face of such apparent reverses, however, de
Gaulle did not alter the fundamental elements in his programme for peace in Europe.   To be sure, the French government made some gestures in the autumn of 1968 indicating a
desire for *rapprochement* with Washington, and underlining its
commitment to the common Western defence.   But the basic
Gaullist tenet that the maintenance of the Eastern and Western
blocs is against the interests of the European nations was firmly
upheld.   Indeed, the French president asserted in his first press
conference after the invasion of Czechoslovakia that if his
policy had been ' momentarily thwarted ', it was nevertheless
' in agreement with profound European realities ' and would
therefore be pursued.[44]   Thus General de Gaulle sought to
escape the dilemma created for him by the occupation of
Czechoslovakia first and foremost by expressing his confidence
that *détente* would prevail in spite of all and that this would
eventually again enable the smaller states of Eastern Europe
to reassert their independence.[45]   At the same time the French
government was anxious to convey unmistakable signals to
Moscow that the only alternative to the road towards *détente*
was a return to the climate of a cold war, and that Paris for its
part was ready to proceed on that road to *détente* as soon as
Moscow had accepted its fundamental premises.[46]   These were
clearly stated by the French foreign minister Michel Debré
early in November 1968 when he declared that *détente* must be
built on liberty and lead to liberty.   He emphasized that a new
relationship between Western Europe and the Soviet Union
based on understanding and co-operation was inseparable
from better relations between the smaller East European
nations and Moscow.   This meant that liberalization of the
Czechoslovak type must be permissible—hence his conclusion
that the basis of *détente* is liberty.[47]
    France's policy towards the East, upset as it was by the
Soviet intervention in Czechoslovakia, had never been explicitly

attacked by Moscow. The Soviet condemnation of West Germany's *Ostpolitik* on the other hand was one of the main elements in Moscow's attempts to justify the invasion. This in itself did not induce Bonn to revise its official stand towards the East, but Chancellor Kiesinger acknowledged that the occupation of Czechoslovakia and the Soviet doctrine of limited sovereignty called for a re-examination of the basic premises in West Germany's Eastern policy. The preliminary conclusion arrived at in the autumn of 1968 reconfirmed not only the previously adopted long-term objective but also the main steps on the road to that ultimate goal. The government therefore decided to continue its search for improved relations with the East European states and the Soviet Union.[48] According to the official interpretation issued by Bonn, the events in Czechoslovakia had complicated West Germany's efforts but they had become more urgent than ever.[49]

While the main elements in the Federal Republic's programme for peace in Europe remained largely unaltered, some of the basic positions relevant to this programme were nevertheless modified in the immediate aftermath of the invasion. It is perhaps indicative of the lack of consonance between the main internal forces determining West German foreign policy that these modifications had different implications. The first change was a ' hardening ' of Bonn's position on intra-German relations: on 26 September 1968 the *Bundestag* adopted a resolution, one point* of which could only be interpreted as an explicit reaffirmation of the Federal Republic's claim to represent the whole of Germany, the so-called *Alleinvertretungsanspruch*.[50] This meant a reversal of a trend to allow this part of West German policy to fade away, a trend which had become established since the Grand Coalition was formed.[51] The other modification, which passed almost unnoticed, was the careful wording in two official declarations on the subject of the Munich agreement of 1938. They came closer to the Soviet and East European position on this issue than any

---

*This point (no. 6) of the resolution was adopted with the concurring votes of the CDU/CSU and the SPD. The FDP of the opposition, having drafted a different formulation which would have preserved the original line of policy on this issue, voted against.

previous West German official pronouncement. Although Mr Brandt still did not subscribe to the Soviet contention that the agreement had been *invalid from the outset*, he now declared that it had been *unjust from the very beginning*, thereby indicating with even greater emphasis than previously that no claims whatsoever could legitimately be based by Bonn on Hitler's *diktat* of 1938.[52]

The announcement of the Soviet theory of limited sovereignty gave the West German process of reappraisal a new impetus. Even though earlier Soviet declarations, including Ambassador Tsarapkin's representations to Chancellor Kiesinger on 2 September 1968,[53] had prepared the ground for this ' doctrine ', its presentation from the august rostrum of the United Nations as a coherent system of policy directives confronted the West German government with a new situation. The interpretation given to this doctrine by responsible spokesmen of the Bonn government indicated that they saw it as an attempt to make Germany's division permanent by raising a barrier to all efforts at overcoming the *status quo* in Central Europe.[54] Thus, the Soviet stand was seen as a direct challenge not only to the long-term goal of West Germany's *Ostpolitik* but also to the medium- and short-term policies by which the goal was to be reached. The Soviet doctrine seemed to block, at least for the time being, any attempt to achieve a European settlement by increasing East–West co-operation and gradually enlarging areas of interest common to countries with different social systems, an indirect approach which had been explicitly endorsed in the joint statement adopted at the Karlovy Vary conference of 1967, and had been the most promising until the autumn of 1968.

The reappraisal of the West German programme for peace in Europe in the light of this modified Soviet stand appeared to imply a temporary pause in Bonn's *Ostpolitik* but no revision of the basic conception of the proper means to be used in future efforts to attain the long-term goal of a European *Friedensordnung*. This result was partly due to the lack of any genuine alternative. It appears also to have been based on two more positive considerations: (1) confidence that the new Soviet doctrine would fade away as the impossibility of imposing **separate standards of** international law on an arbitrarily defined group of states revealed itself,[55] and (2) the trend towards expanding the international division of labour and the prospect that enlightened self-interest would eventually induce the Soviet Union to permit this extension to grow beyond the limits of the socialist community.[56]

There remains the question of how the invasion of Czechoslovakia impinged upon Moscow's programme for peace in Europe and upon those of its East European allies. We have earlier noted that the collective long-term objectives agreed upon at Bucharest and Karlovy Vary in 1966 and 1967 were reconfirmed by Soviet government spokesmen in the autumn of 1968.[57] The same is true of the step towards peace in Europe most favoured by the Soviet Union: the convening of a conference of all European states to discuss questions relating to the safeguarding of security and the development of pan-European co-operation. Both the collective programme and the conference proposals were repeated in Foreign Minister Gromyko's speech before the Supreme Soviet on 27 June 1968; they were referred to again in the joint statement adopted at the Bratislava conference on 3 August 1968 and finally reconfirmed by Mr Gromyko in his speech before the United Nations on 3 October 1968. Yet there were some peculiarities in the way in which the Soviet position was presented (on this last occasion) after the occupation of Czechoslovakia. In his address Mr Gromyko explicitly endorsed, even encouraged, continued and extended *bilateral* contacts between East and West European states, but this portion of his speech did not appear in the issue of *Pravda* which claimed to reproduce the full text.[58] This was perhaps a hint that Moscow intended to impose a strict control over the relations of its East European allies with the West, an issue which the doctrine of limited sovereignty, enunciated in the same speech, raised in a broader and more fundamental sense. Henceforth it was unclear how much latitude, if any, would be given to the ruling élites in these states to determine not only their relations with the non-communist world but also the character of their own societies. Yet it had been a basic assumption in the West that prospects for peace in Europe depended to a large extent on the answer to this question. The reactions in the course of the autumn of 1968 from East

Berlin, Warsaw, Bucharest, and Budapest indicated that this was indeed a very 'hot' issue.

The leaders of the German Democratic Republic endorsed most emphatically the new Soviet thesis about the implications of 'socialist internationalism'. Mr Ulbricht welcomed Foreign Minister Gromyko's declaration to the United Nations General Assembly that the Soviet Union would never permit any single state to be prized loose from the community of socialist states.[59] The East German foreign minister, Mr Winzer, denounced the concepts of 'abstract and class-indifferent' sovereignty and self-determination as 'bourgeois aberrations', and repeated the 'correct' interpretation of socialist international law.[60] In addition he clearly spelled out the policy which would have to follow from giving priority to the principle of socialist internationalism. He asserted that the strengthening of the socialist order in each individual socialist country as well as the cohesion of the socialist camp as a whole were the *preconditions* for a successful struggle to realize the principles of peaceful coexistence in relations with the capitalist world. 'Peaceful coexistence' in turn was described in most militant terms as a strategy that would permit the united economic, political, and military forces of the socialist states in Europe to rebuff the machinations of West German and American imperialism and to *enforce* the establishment of a peaceful system of European security. Thus, the consolidation of the socialist camp was now presented by the GDR as the first and foremost requirement for peace in Europe.

Poland's Wladyslaw Gomulka also subscribed to the validity of the recent Soviet interpretation of 'socialist internationalism'. In a major address on 11 October 1968 he spoke disapprovingly of certain communist parties which 'took towards the August events a stand from the position of an abstractly-conceived sovereignty'.[61] Mr Gomulka, who had come to power in 1956 as a staunch advocate of the thesis about different roads to socialism, declared that while the roads to socialism might be different there was only *one* socialism.[62] This assertion left crucial questions unanswered: what were the criteria for 'true' socialism, and who was to decide whether a certain line of development in a socialist country threatened to violate the fundamental principles of socialism? The invasion of Czechoslovakia had demonstrated that Moscow was determined to remain the sole arbiter of these basic issues. It may have been exactly because Mr Gomulka realized this and knew that Moscow could permit deviations in Poland no more—or even less—than in Czechoslovakia, that he seems to have been groping for some general principles which would prevent complete arbitrariness on the part of the Soviet Union by limiting the scope for ' legitimate ' intervention in the affairs of individual East European states. When Mr Gomulka called for a ' deep ideological discussion ' in order to promote normalization in Czechoslovakia, he very likely had in mind a normalization of relations between Warsaw and Moscow also, since they cannot have remained unaffected by ' the August events '. The Polish leader insisted that an answer must be given to the question: what is common to the building of socialism in all countries, and what is specific for individual countries? [63] Upon the resolution of these fundamental issues depended the extent to which the Polish leadership would be free to develop its own society and bi-lateral relations with the non-communist world.

The Polish reservations about the new Soviet stand on relations amongst socialist states were cautious hints at most. Those emanating from Bucharest on the other hand were straightforward and explicit.* In a major speech on 29 November 1968 Mr Ceausescu minced no words on the subject of the Soviet doctrine when he asserted:

The thesis attempted to get accredited of late, and according to which the joint defence of the socialist countries against an imperialist attack would presuppose limitation or renunciation of the sover-eignty of any [Warsaw] Treaty member-state does not accord with the principles of relationship between the socialist countries and can by no means be accepted. Not only does membership in the Warsaw Treaty not render questionable the sovereignty of the member-countries, not only does it not ' limit ' in any way their state inde-pendence, but on the contrary, as provided for in the Treaty itself,

*The official attitude of Czechoslovakia to the Soviet doctrine of limited sovereignty has not been included in this preliminary analysis of early East Euro-pean reactions because of the special situation in that country since Aug. 1968. Bulgaria in general followed the Soviet line.

it serves for strengthening of the independence and national sovereignty of each state.[64]

If Mr Gomulka had called for a discussion among the communist parties in order to arrive at some joint principles of socialist construction and thus to clarify how much freedom the different ruling parties retained to travel separate roads to socialism, there seemed to be no doubt in Mr Ceausescu's mind on these basic issues.

Socialism cannot be but one [he declared] and it is characterized by the socialization of the means of production and by the achievement of a society in which both the political power and the means of production belong to the working class, to the people. *This is the essential condition, the decisive criterion, on the basis of which it can be assessed whether a country is socialist or not and not any other considerations invented at the desk, divorced from life and from reality.*[65]

This was clear language. The implicit criticism against Soviet behaviour in Czechoslovakia and the warning against the consequences of similar moves against Rumania were unmistakable when later in his speech Mr Ceausescu declared:

Any interference in the internal affairs of another party, an act of supporting groups or isolated members of other parties are not only of no help to the respective party, but on the contrary, lead to weakening its unity and consequently are incompatible with the internationalist relations among parties. In these conditions, each party has the right and duty to take every measure it deems necessary to defend its unity and cohesion, to strengthen its fighting capacity.[66]

The pronouncements of the Rumanian leadership were significant not only because they rejected Moscow's hegemonic claim but also because they showed that only three months after the invasion of Czechoslovakia the leaders in Bucharest saw fit to reassert their basic views with regard to the proper steps leading to peace in Europe. While Moscow and its allies in East Berlin and Warsaw emphasized the danger from the imperialists and their new techniques of ' peaceful counter-revolution ', the Rumanian communist leader cautioned against ' any over-estimation or exaggeration of the strength of reaction and imperialism ', which could lead only to ' panic, to mistrust in the capacity of the anti-imperialist front of rejecting and defeating the aggressive imperialist actions '. Only a few weeks after the Soviet party leader, Mr Brezhnev, had emphasized the importance of strengthening the military apparatus of the WTO,[67] his Rumanian colleague declared that ' peace, security and *détente* cannot be achieved by consolidating military blocs, but by abolishing them, by placing inter-state relations on sound bases of cooperation and mutual confidence '. Pursuing this line of thought, he called for new steps ' along the road of economic, political, technical, and scientific cooperation, of political negotiations, of *détente* ' among the peoples of the European continent.[68]

While Bucharest sought to safeguard its limited independence by rejecting the Soviet doctrine, Budapest chose a less drastic procedure—it denied the existence of any new doctrine. In a remarkable lecture delivered on 11 December 1968 the Hungarian foreign minister, Mr Janos Peter, spoke about a ' NATO theory ' that ' some sort of a new doctrine ' had been developed and applied by the socialist countries.[69] Attributing this ' theory ' to the mistranslation of a Russian term used by Mr Gromyko in his speech before the United Nations, the Hungarian foreign minister asserted that there was no new doctrine but only an old one, which stated that the course of history could not be reversed: where socialism had triumphed it had triumphed definitively. Mr Peter did not address himself to the unpleasant issues bothering Mr Gomulka and Mr Ceausescu about the proper criteria of socialism, but the implicit conclusion of his argument was the same as that pronounced explicitly by Mr Ceausescu, namely, that there were no limitations to the sovereign right of each socialist country to determine its own road to socialism. Mr Peter acknowledged that following 21 August 1968 and what he euphemistically chose to call ' the involvement of the five allied socialist countries ' in Czechoslovakia, international relations in Europe had deteriorated. He blamed the NATO countries for increasing international tension, but, using an argument similar to that presented by Mr Ceausescu about the fundamental balance of forces being in favour of the socialist states, he argued that the main task was to prevent the NATO measures from blocking the road to a new security system in Europe based on the co-operation of European countries with different social systems.

If in the aftermath of the invasion of Czechoslovakia the East German leaders were emphasizing the need to step up the consolidation of the socialist camp, Mr Peter expressed a contrary view to the effect that the process of consolidation in Czechoslovakia had strengthened the socialist countries sufficiently for them to launch new initiatives for peace, security, and co-operation in Europe.* In essence, the speech of the Hungarian foreign minister, like that of Mr Ceausescu, implied a plea that the forces of *détente* be revived in spite of events in Czechoslovakia.

It is uncertain what impact the Rumanian and Hungarian arguments had on official views in the Soviet capital. But there were soon indications that the Soviet leadership was willing to acquiesce in a more flexible approach towards the West in Europe. The appeal issued by the Warsaw Pact countries in connection with a meeting of their leaders in Budapest on 17 March 1969, which included a call for a European security conference, was couched in a distinctly conciliatory tone.[70] Among the preconditions to be fulfilled in order to safeguard peace in Europe, the appeal mentioned 'the recognition of the *existence* of the GDR', [71] not its recognition as a sovereign state according to established rules of international law. This formula seemed to leave open the possibility of a *rapprochement* between Bonn and East Berlin.[72] Similarly, in the spring of 1969, there were signs of less hostile Polish attitudes towards West Germany. This was particularly reflected in Mr Gomulka's proposal to conclude a border agreement with the Federal Republic, which did not include previous demands for a *simultaneous* recognition of the GDR.[73]

Did Moscow allow these new signals of conciliation merely for tactical reasons, to repair the severe damage that the image of the Soviet Union as a 'peace-loving' power had suffered throughout the world as a result of the events in

---

*This difference in perspective cannot be attributed to developments which had occurred in Czechoslovakia between October (when the East German declarations on which our analysis is based were issued) and the time of Mr Peter's lecture. 'Consolidation' in Czechoslovakia had hardly made significant progress during Nov. and early Dec. 1968.

Czechoslovakia? Or was this acquiescence a harbinger of a shift in the priorities of Soviet foreign policy? In the light of the evidence available at the time of writing, it seemed that the Czechoslovak crisis would come to be regarded not only as the end of one phase but also as the beginning of another.

PROSPECTS FOR PEACE IN EUROPE: THE REQUIREMENTS FOR A BETTER MODUS VIVENDI AND FOR AN ULTIMATE SETTLEMENT

IN spite of severe setbacks in the past and the slight chances of success in the near future, the search for a European settlement must continue. So much is now spent to keep the confrontation in precarious balance and so much would be at stake if that balance were lost that some positive improvement in the present situation is clearly imperative.

There are two elements to the *risks* involved in the Central European confrontation: the likelihood of war breaking out and the stakes involved if it did. Since Europe remains the geographical area where the greatest destructive potential is concentrated and firm commitments of both superpowers are involved, the possibility of escalation if an armed conflict broke out there raises the spectre of Armageddon. This very fact has tended to deter the main actors from rash actions and thus to decrease the likelihood of war. Yet the possibility of an all-devastating conflict remains as long as the contenders in the world arena have the means of destruction at their disposal. Even if the danger of irrational acts is discounted, the behaviour of states is subject to the pressures and constraints of powerful social, economic, and political forces, the net effects of which are never fully controllable by governments nor predictable by analysts.

At present, there are partly muted yet dynamic forces of change at work on both sides of the dividing line in Europe. In the East there is an increase in articulate pressure for greater economic efficiency, the decentralization of political power, and the protection of basic civil rights. The ruling élites, anxious to preserve their monopoly of power, may be able to contain these forces by repression for some time, but they are unlikely to be quenched for good, and might spark off an upheaval which, if uncontrolled, could develop into an international crisis. In the West, there is also the danger that a tendency towards ossification of the political system will result in the alienation of large groups frustrated by the inability of policy-makers to cope adequately with the urgent problems besetting industrial and post-industrial societies. This in turn could erode the sense of common purpose and solidarity in the West to a point where the continued viability and credibility of the Western alliance would be seriously endangered, thus engendering new fears and instabilities. Even on the dividing line itself, the uncertain dynamics of German affairs and the potential explosiveness of the basic issues provide sufficient grounds for concern about the stability of the present structure.[1]

The *costs* of the East–West confrontation in Central Europe must be measured not only by the expenditure of the major powers in maintaining defence postures, but also by the wastage of scarce human resources. The division of Europe has become a monument to the inability of East and West to co-operate with each other, but for the world as a whole, this co-operation is essential to solve the less politically acute but in the long run much more serious problems confronting mankind in the age of science and technology.

Given the intractability of the issues dividing East and West in Europe on the one hand, and the trend towards increasing interdependence between highly developed countries on the other, our best hope for an ultimate settlement in Europe may still lie in the realization by both sides that their common interests are infinitely more important than their traditional differences and conflicts. The latter part of this chapter is devoted to speculations about the admittedly difficult road to that long-term goal. First, however, we shall attempt to formulate in the light of recent experience some of the requirements for the humbler yet crucial task of bringing about a better *modus vivendi* between East and West in Europe, which could at the same time provide a basis for an ultimate settlement.

In search of a better modus vivendi

Any attempt to formulate the requirements for better East–West relations in Europe must begin with an understanding of the perspectives in which the main countries have regarded the prevailing power balance in Europe.

Western Europe. The predominance of the Soviet Union on the European continent has been considered in Western Europe as a threat which could be effectively contained only through some kind of association with the United States. Although political consolidation and economic growth and integration in Western Europe, together with a less aggressive Soviet posture towards the West, have significantly diminished West European fears and the concomitant feelings of dependence on America, the need for some ultimate reassurance from the United States remains vital to all West European countries for the foreseeable future.

The Soviet Union. For the Soviet Union as a world power, Europe has primarily been a theatre of direct confrontation with its main contender in world politics, the United States. Western Europe has constituted both a buffer-zone against the United States and a hostage to ensure good behaviour from the Americans. The overriding Soviet interests in Europe have therefore been to secure firm control over Eastern Europe and to prevent the emergence of a closely knit Atlantic combination which would hold the preponderance of power on the continent. Consolidation in Eastern and Central Europe on Soviet terms, the fragmentation of Western Europe, and the loosening of American ties with Western Europe have been and are likely to remain the standard Soviet prescriptions for peace and security in Europe.

The United States. The defence of Western Europe will continue to be a primary American interest in the 1970s but the reasons for this will probably be economic, psychological, and sentimental rather than strategic. Contrary to the situation of the late 1950s, the United States today is hardly dependent on the co-operation of Western Europe to maintain a crude balance of power with the Soviet Union and its allies, however one chooses to define such a balance. Thus American interests would seem to dictate a policy which would not allow that region to fall under Soviet domination, which would retain sufficient leverage in Europe to prevent a development that might involve America in a major conflict with Russia, and which would encourage close contacts with the Soviet leadership in order to keep any dispute in Central Europe within manageable bounds.

Eastern Europe. Eastern Europe has neither the political weight nor the cohesion of the regions previously discussed. To the extent that the interests of these countries coincide—which is only limited—there is a precarious balancing between the wish to seek greater independence from Soviet tutelage and the necessity to pay due regard to Soviet security interests, between the desire to utilize contacts with the West for economic development and technological innovation and the need for some Soviet backing against the threat of Western domination.

A critique of Western policy

Because of the incongruence of interests and power relations between the states of these four regions and the combination of brittleness and high stakes which characterizes the confrontation in Central Europe, alternative constellations can come about only gradually over a long period of time. Furthermore, it must not be assumed that solutions to the intractable issues besetting Central Europe will emerge simply as the casual product of the play between semi-autonomous forces. To achieve conditions that will be conducive to greater stability and East–West accommodation, these forces will have to be consciously and consistently utilized by those wielding political power. In view of the Soviet preference to formalize prevailing conditions in Central Europe and the Western aspiration to change the *status quo*, the need to elaborate new schemes that would take into account the legitimate interests of all concerned will probably be felt more strongly in the West. This is the main reason for concentrating our discussion on future options of the Western powers. If, however, we are to minimize the possibility of new frustrations, we must learn from the shortcomings in Western performance during the last few years.

Unfortunately, these have been obscured by Soviet intransigence and brutality in the Czechoslovak crisis. Nevertheless, it is one thing to maintain that the frame of mind of the

Soviet leaders foreclosed any chance for East–West agreements that did not simply imply accepting Moscow's demands, and quite another to argue that Western policies offered a reasonable basis for continued *rapprochement* and eventual accommodation with the East. Given the over-all military resources, economic dynamism, and technological superiority of the West, even a Soviet government less obsessed than the present one with the dangers of ideological infection would probably have viewed Western efforts aimed at overcoming the division of Europe with great concern. Two kinds of measures could make these policies more acceptable to the USSR, namely: (1) a tangible offer of significant modifications in Western politico-military postures; and (2) credible reassurances about the non-interventionist nature of Western designs in Eastern Europe. While many responsible spokesmen in the West realized that overcoming the division of Europe must entail fundamental changes in alliance structures and expressed themselves to that effect, no Western leader was able to do more than hint at such possible rearrangements on the European continent.[2]

As the analysis in chapter 1 indicates, the lack of a clear-cut Western position was essentially due to conflicting aspirations and expectations in the West with regard to the future shape of Europe and its relations with the superpowers. It is true that reassurances about Western schemes in Eastern Europe were given, but they certainly lacked consistency. By 1966, the American government had explicitly disavowed all intention of subverting communist governments in Eastern Europe or enticing any East European country away from the Soviet Union.[3] At the same time, however, some leading West German officials expressed themselves in terms which were either clearly incompatible or at least difficult to reconcile with this policy.[4] This contradictoriness in Western positions was further compounded by the ambiguity in West Germany's official stand on the German question as part of the ultimate goal of the new *Ostpolitik*.[5] The Kiesinger-Brandt government felt constrained from expounding authoritatively the long-term aim of a European peace order by differences of view between the two main coalition partners. Consequently, official West

German statements relating to this central theme were not fully consistent.[6]

The Soviet Union has exploited the lack of clarity in the Western stand for propaganda purposes.[7]   This, however, should not obscure its inherent flaws.   In essence, the Soviet Union was confronted with a Western policy whose avowed aim was to change the *status quo* in Central Europe.   Even though the West had issued repeated assurances that this goal would be sought only by peaceful means, the implications of its aspirations were shrouded in ambiguous formulas like ' the European peace order '.   At the same time, there was ample evidence to suggest that influential spokesmen in the West were calculating on a process the end result of which would be the reunification of Germany within the framework of the Atlantic alliance.[8]   No conceivable Russian government could view such an idea with anything but apprehension.

The main deficiency in the Western position towards the East during the period under review consisted in the fact that a policy ostensibly aiming at reconciliation lacked sufficient clarity and consistency to be credible to the East.   The force of this contention is not weakened by the fact that during this particular period the sincerity of Western policies was never properly tested by the East European governments because of the excessively fearful and defensive attitudes of the Kremlin. The shortcomings in past Western performance suggest some definite measures required to bring about a more effective Western policy.

Suggestions for a modified Western stand

If it is true that one of the necessary conditions for an accommodation with the East is greater uniformity in Western policies, then efforts to improve Western co-operation are of primary importance.   It is suggested that this view may reasonably be accepted even by those who have earlier argued that the greatest concentration of energies be devoted to the amelioration of East–West relations since it now seems clear that the goal they favour can be achieved only when the West has developed a greater sense of common purpose.   But the formulation of a co-ordinated Western policy towards the East cannot be postponed until relations in the West have been revitalized. The two are interrelated and must be undertaken simultaneously.

In the search for greater Western unity, what are the guidelines that would take into account the requirements of a future settlement with the East? From the foregoing analysis of Western and Eastern policies during 1966–8, it would seem that three are essential. The first would be to guarantee Western Europe against Soviet domination. The second guideline should be to show the Soviet Union convincingly that speculating in the ultimate disruption of Western cohesion is unprofitable. The third would be to give the Soviet Union less reason to fear the growth of autonomy in the East European states.

Success in forging any Western configuration satisfying these three basic requirements will mainly hinge on the way in which two central issues are managed: the nature of America's commitments to Europe, and the politico-military posture of the Federal Republic.

Efforts to bring about a new viable relationship between America and Europe will have to take into account mounting domestic pressures in the United States for a reduced American military presence in Europe. This trend appears to be virtually irreversible unless some unforeseeable drastic deterioration in relations between the superpowers should occur. At the same time, the facilities for rapid and massive movement of military personnel over long distances are likely to improve, and it may be reasonable to expect that the adverse psychological impact of ' Big Lift ' techniques and troop rotating procedures in Western defence practices could at least partly be offset by a process of mutual education and adaptation.[9] Yet the West European allies of the United States are likely to insist on an American presence that is more than symbolic. In the case of West Germany, this will primarily be due to a residual and possibly recurring concern lest an emerging military preponderance in the East be used to undermine the stability of the Federal Republic. Many other West European states, anxious to preserve American backing against Russia, are apt to feel uneasy lest an American disengagement from

Europe might make them excessively dependent on West Germany. Thus whatever the future arrangements for West European defence are going to be, an American commitment appears crucial not only to provide the necessary counter-vailing power against the Soviet Union, but also the focal point for co-ordinated defence efforts in Western Europe.

America's commitment is also essential in order to meet the second guide-line. Soviet hopes for American disengagement from Europe will have to be dashed before Moscow is likely to show genuine interest in co-operating with the United States to find a more acceptable *modus vivendi* in Europe. This does not necessarily imply a preference for any one formula of West European or transatlantic co-operation, but it does confront the West with the task of forging intra-alliance relations in such a way as to convey a more credible image of long-term solidarity. Otherwise, it will still be impossible to prevent the Soviet Union from following a selective *détente* policy towards the West, the first signs of which became visible soon after the invasion of Czechoslovakia.[10] Such a Western posture may well have to await a more advanced stage in West European co-operation, possibly including British participation in the EEC, and it certainly presupposes that the United States will recover its sense of purpose and confidence, so patently lacking at the end of the 1960s.

Since, for the reasons mentioned above, the United States will probably reduce the number of troops it has in Europe, the traditional way of indicating a political commitment by local military presence will have to be complemented. The Western nations should explore together how, other than by the joint deployment of military forces, they can credibly demonstrate their basic and continuing community of interest and purpose. New co-operative patterns among the West European countries alone could prevent the inevitable reduction of the American presence in Europe from jeopardizing the image of Western solidarity. Thus, under the umbrella of the alliance with the United States, overlapping combinations might evolve which could eventually bring about a situation where NATO would no longer appear as the only focus of Western cohesion and defence.[11]

But if ultimately some form of American engagement in
Europe remains a *sine qua non* for a viable Western posture,
what scope is there for rearrangements in the West that could
offer some reassurance to Moscow and thus make it easier for
the USSR to loosen the reins in Eastern Europe? Historically
the military capacity and political stance of Germany have
been of crucial significance for Soviet policy in Europe and they
will probably remain so. Any government in Bonn concerned
about reconciliation with the East will have to adopt obviously
non-provocative military dispositions and a conciliatory
political stand.

The size and structure of West Germany's armed forces
have generally been recognized as a critical factor in all
schemes for arms control and political accommodation in
Central Europe. Yet the specific dilemma confronting the
Federal Republic is not always understood. Given present
force levels and political trends in the East it must remain a
primary West German interest to make sure that Western
defence arrangements immediately affecting the Federal
Republic should not be easily exploitable as evidence of
' German aggressiveness ' nor liable to bring about an erosion
of deterrence. The question of which specific mix of defence
dispositions would best satisfy these requirements, which are
difficult to reconcile, has been the subject of lively debate in
the *Bundestag** and elsewhere, centring particularly on West
German participation in NATO's nuclear strike force.[12]
Because West German defence planning is based on the
elaborate Western system of deterrence as it is at present, in
which West German weapons acquisition has been geared to
producing nuclear delivery vehicles,[13] Bonn cannot be expected
to abandon its present policy easily. But to the extent that
reassuring the East is accorded high priority by the Federal
Republic, it would seem to be in the interest of West Germany
to divest its armed forces of all functions connected with
nuclear deterrence. The adoption of such a demonstratively

*It is worth noting that the main SPD spokesman in these debates pleaded for
greater emphasis on a conventional option for the West German air force yet
supported Defence Minister Schröder's basic contention that deterrence required
continued West German participation in the nuclear strike force.

non-offensive military posture, however, is complicated by the French policy of status improvement based to a significant extent on France's nuclear armaments. Thus, a West German military stand fully adapted to the requirements of accommodation with the East may have to await the time when the nuclear forces of both Britain and France have become obsolete and the search for West European political and defence co-operation has reached more conclusive and tangible results.

If modification of the *military* component is thus likely to be inhibited for some time by a number of circumstances, external as well as domestic, what are the prospects for a change in the *political* stand of the Federal Republic that would help to reassure the East? The main task here is to find in co-operation with the other Western allies and with due regard to West Germany's fragile political structure a new position that would unambiguously accept two features of the present territorial and political *status quo* in Europe: (1) the Oder-Neisse line as Poland's western border, and (2) the existence of the GDR as a political reality and its leadership as an equal partner in any scheme aiming at the improvement of East–West relations in Europe.

Proposing the elaboration of a common Western position on these issues does not imply that agreements on them should be offered to the Eastern powers without some commitments in exchange. We shall discuss these further below. At this point we only wish to emphasize the importance of clarifying the Western stand. There is no assurance—indeed, in the short run it seems most unlikely—that such clarification could by itself induce the Soviet Union to relax its grip on Eastern Europe. It is nevertheless a necessary step in order to eliminate residual East European apprehensions of West Germany and the opportunity they give for the USSR to use the West German bogy as a means of consolidating the Soviet sphere of influence. Only in these circumstances is it conceivable that the East European states will be able to assert their autonomy without arousing alarm in Moscow, and thus that the stage for a new round of East–West *rapprochement* can be set.

The question of relations between the West and East Germany has been bedevilled by confusion about the implication of ' recognizing ' East Germany. Partly intentionally, the distinction has been blurred between, on the one hand, legitimizing the East German regime as democratically instituted and, on the other, establishing normal relations with East Berlin in accordance with recognized legal rules.[14] When in the following we argue that some form of recognition will be necessary to achieve a qualitative improvement of conditions in Central Europe the term is used only in the latter sense.

Quite apart from the present opposition in West Germany to any *de jure* recognition of the GDR as a separate state, it would be to disregard the dynamics of intra-German relations if one were to suggest that a step in this direction be taken by Bonn and its allies unilaterally and in isolation from other issues.

The problem of the proper *form* of relations between the FRG and the GDR cannot be separated from the *substance* of these relations, and the latter in turn can only be tackled effectively in the context of a mutual redefinition of official positions in both East and West.[15] Any such scheme will have to be elaborated within a wider framework of East–West accommodation in Europe but must at the same time take into account the complementary instabilities within East and West Germany, due mainly to the potentially disruptive repercussions of intra-German relations.[16] The simple act of ' recognizing ' the GDR is therefore no panacea for better East–West relations in Europe—although some form of recognition will be a necessary element in a strategy aiming at this goal. If Bonn were to recognize East Germany at a time when the government in East Berlin had reason to fear that this step was taken to undermine its power position, the result would hardly benefit intra-German *rapprochement*. The same holds true of a recognition wrung from a West German government under international pressure without any assurance that the East was willing to pay the price that every West German government will have to insist upon: more humane conditions along the dividing-line and particularly in Berlin. Yet the security of the political system in East Germany and the survival of the ruling élite must not be threatened by Western policy (explicitly or implicitly). Only then will it be reasonable to expect the

East German leadership to let its genuine interest in the evolution of economic ties with the West, and especially with West Germany, take the upper hand.[17]

Moreover, the indigenous forces in Eastern Europe striving for a *rapprochement* will be able to prevail only when Soviet supremacy is not directly challenged by Western policy. This point should not be understood as a plea for a formal sphere-of-influence agreement with Moscow. Quite the opposite: that approach would not hold out great hope for a more workable *modus vivendi* in Europe, precisely because it is unlikely that Soviet coercion will in the long run be able to safeguard stable conditions in Eastern Europe. But the degree to which the Soviet Union is going to tolerate, and the ruling East European leaders will venture to embark upon, new departures in East–West co-operation will depend largely on whether Moscow can credibly associate the forces of change in Eastern Europe with a Western policy it could depict as subversive. During the period under review the main example of such a policy was the West German effort to ' overcome ' the *status quo* without clarifying fully the implications.

The Western posture most conducive to allowing gradual and cautious change to mature in Eastern Europe without undue risk of a Soviet clamp-down would be one which emphasized the readiness of the West to co-operate with any country in the East, without challenging Soviet predominance in the area. This does not mean that the West would have to acquiesce passively in whatever actions the Soviet leadership might wish to take in order to contain the efforts of an East European state seeking greater independence. But Western means of dissuading Moscow from brutal behaviour in Eastern Europe are distinctly limited. The United States could make representations to Moscow about the possible repercussions such acts might have on issues of arms control and armaments policy, and, in addition, perhaps give some indication of the risks of escalation once force were again used in Europe.[18] But since the Western powers will not risk war, one cannot regard as realistic any suggestion that the West would collectively and forcefully defend the right of East European states to shape their own destiny.[19] Thus the best prescription for

Western policy towards Eastern Europe may still be one that is guided by Averell Harriman's assertion in 1967 that ' progress [towards peace in Europe] depends in no small degree on the development of more open societies in the East'; that ' these changes can only come from within, but . . . can be encouraged by our readiness to co-operate '.[20]

As already indicated, the suggested revision of Western postures can be the result only of a package deal involving amendment and reformulation of policy positions in the East as well. The demand for the recognition of East Germany has been put forward by Moscow and East Berlin in a fashion that has been construed by Bonn as an attempt to undermine the stability of the FRG. These Eastern governments for their part will therefore have to give up the claim of a right to intervene in West German society on the basis of the Potsdam Agreement of 1945 if the impasse is to be overcome and the road cleared for some form of recognition.[21]

However, the requirement that the demand for the recognition of East Germany be divested of all interventionist overtones strikes at the core of Soviet policy in Europe, for the manipulation of the German question, including the threat of intervention in West Germany, has constituted one of the most important instruments in Moscow's attempts to break the backbone of the Western alliance, ' the Bonn-Washington axis '. Giving up this lever would therefore ultimately mean that Moscow would accept a redefinition of peaceful coexistence in Europe more in line with Western conceptions of its implications. One factor which could influence Moscow is the attitude of the other East European states. These countries would seem to have an interest in viewing the recognition of the GDR as a necessary precondition for pan-European co-operative schemes rather than as the first step towards the ' democratization ' of West Germany.[22]

Along with the renunciation of this interventionist option must come guarantees for the viability of West Berlin which could be an element in a deal to normalize intra-German relations and formalize the acceptance of existing borders in Central Europe by all parties concerned. Here again the interests of the Eastern powers do not coincide. Poland,

Czechoslovakia, and Hungary—not to speak of Rumania and Bulgaria—have a positive interest in keeping tensions in Berlin at a low level. The Soviet Union and East Germany, on the other hand, have repeatedly used the exposed position of West Berlin to put pressure on the Western powers. Thus, an agreement on West Berlin would ultimately require a re-orientation of Moscow's policy, with the result that one of its main tools, the potential for generating crises in Berlin, would be discarded.

On negotiating procedures

It is one thing to suggest or recognize necessary modifications of present policy positions, and quite another to bring them about. Indeed, the problem of reaching some substantive agreement between East and West in Europe is made distinctly more difficult by procedural complications. We shall now briefly review four alternative negotiating schemes and attempt to assess some of their pros and cons, keeping in mind that the objective of negotiations should be a better *modus vivendi* which at the same time would provide a basis for an ultimate settlement.

SALT. Although we do not know what issues may be dealt with on the margin of the Soviet-American strategic arms limitation talks (dubbed SALT), their bipolar structure and distinctly circumscribed formal substance does not suggest that they could be a proper framework for dealing effectively with the problems of Europe's future. At best, SALT could facilitate arms control measures that reflect a limited community of interests between the United States and the Soviet Union. Such steps may be of significance for conditions in Central Europe, but they cannot by themselves stimulate the necessary sense of common purpose and a willingness to compromise among all the main parties concerned.

Negotiations between NATO and the WTO. This framework could be useful for negotiations on regional arms control measures but much less so for dealing with political issues. The major objection against this setting is the fact that it would prejudge the substantive outcome of negotiations, since the predominance of the superpowers in each part of Europe would be emphasized. This, however, is contrary to the aspirations not only of France but also of most of the Soviet allies in Eastern Europe, although they have been less outspoken on the subject.

Bilateral negotiations between individual countries in East and West. Such talks and contacts can undoubtedly be helpful and their multiplication should be encouraged. It is true that some of the most intricate and crucial questions—such as the modalities for some sort of German unification and arms control measures in Central Europe—require by their very nature negotiations within a multilateral framework. However, even these issues could be brought significantly closer to a solution through bilateral negotiations. This is specifically true of contacts between Bonn on the one hand and Moscow, Warsaw, and East Berlin on the other. In a *short and medium range perspective* the extension of bilateral talks across the dividing-line could therefore provide useful preparation and eventually a propitious environment for multilateral negotiations within the framework of a European security conference.*

A European Security Conference (ESC). In the course of recent years the Soviet Union and its allies have repeatedly put forward the proposal to convene a European security conference. Prior to 1969 these suggestions were met with a great amount of scepticism by the main Western powers, primarily because they feared that this framework for East–West negotiations would prejudge some of the central issues in any future agreement. To some extent this fear was justified since Moscow advanced its proposal in a way that would promote two basic goals of Soviet foreign policy in Europe: to formalize the *status quo* in Central Europe through *de jure* recognition of East Germany, and to loosen America's ties with Europe through the construction of an exclusively ' European ' negotiating body.[23] During the period under review, the situation changed due to developments in both East and West. In West Germany the idea of recognizing the GDR as an equal partner in negotiations for an East–West *rapprochement* gained ground.[24] Thus the acceptance of the GDR in a European security conference on

---

*In addition, an extending web of bilateral negotiations between East and West can also be seen in *a long range perspective*: as an effort to bring about new patterns of interaction which may eventually be conducive to a major transformation of political and social structures in Europe.

a level of full parity with the FRG would probably no longer have significant unsettling repercussions in West German politics, even if the conference failed to bring German unification perceptibly closer. As indicated above, in the Budapest appeal of spring 1969 the Eastern powers did not insist on *de jure* recognition of the GDR in connection with the convening of a conference.[25] In addition, Moscow seemed willing to accept the participation of the United States and Canada in such a conference from its outset.[26] Under these circumstances, the legitimate Western fears of prejudging substantive issues by accepting the European security conference proposal would seem to have been significantly diminished, and its advantages are therefore worth emphasizing.

Since the GDR would participate in the ESC on equal terms, it would be possible to overcome the main procedural difficulty that has plagued earlier negotiations for European security. While it is unrealistic to assume rapid progress toward agreements, the ESC could provide opportunities for common interests among powers on both sides of the dividing-line to be more generally recognized without causing immediate anxieties on the part of their respective allies. If these conferences were to meet regularly, they would probably eliminate the international isolation of the GDR and enlarge the scope for diplomatic manoeuvres and initiatives of East and West European countries. Both developments are essential if the present impasse is to be overcome.

Finally, the establishment of an ESC *as an institution* could by itself contribute to creating a less explosive situation in Central Europe, especially if its seat were to be Berlin. Under these circumstances, a gradual normalization of conditions in the heart of Germany's previous capital—and possibly elsewhere along the dividing line—would seem to be a natural consequence.

The main advantage of the ESC from the Soviet point of view lies in the fact that the participation of the GDR on equal terms could legitimately be interpreted as symbolizing a major step towards acceptance of the present *status quo* by the West. This in itself should not be a reason for the West to oppose the conference. Indeed, the ESC could prove a vehicle for solving the basic Western dilemma: the need to recognize the *status quo* and yet to initiate a process which would open up some chances for its qualitative transformation. This, however, presupposes that the ESC would not be a one-time show.

Is there a framework for East–West reconciliation?

The preceding analysis has been based on the assumption that in the immediate future—perhaps the next two or three years—the prospects for a qualitative change of conditions in Europe do not seem promising and that all one can reasonably strive for is to hedge against developments that would endanger the present precarious *modus vivendi* in Central Europe; that at an intermediate stage—stretching perhaps over the next decade —there may be both need and opportunity to transform and improve East–West relations in a way that would be conducive to an ultimate settlement; and that this long-term goal, representing the final stage in a process of *rapprochement*, can at best be attained in a time perspective of decades. We have attempted to set out some of the requirements that seem crucial for a move from the first stage to the second. In this concluding section we shall probe into the even more uncertain area of long-term perspectives and set out some of the characteristics of a system that could justifiably be called a peaceful order in Europe. In such an analysis two things must be emphasized: first, we have distinguished different stages in future East–West relations for the sake of focusing attention on different time perspectives. In reality, developments can never be expected to match such analytical abstractions. Second, the formulation of requirements—which essentially means suggesting a specific order of priorities for future action—cannot be undertaken in the abstract but must be related to some notion about probabilities. To a certain extent this has been done in our preceding discussion, but as we embark upon long-term speculations, it is essential that these expectations be spelled out more consistently.

What can we reasonably postulate with regard to future developments in the United States, Europe, and the Soviet Union? With issues of economic efficiency, technological development, and social justice being accorded top priority in most developed countries, what can be assumed about the setting for the performance of the main actors in the East–West drama ? The following crude generalizations are only meant to provide the hypothetical background for some policy suggestions relating to the ultimate issues of peace in Europe.

In view of the complexity of all advanced societies and the many contradictory tendencies in American life in the late 1960s, it is impossible to make any assertion about present and foreseeable conditions in the United States to which some contrary evidence cannot be found. This risk, which has to be run if we are to make any assumptions that can be used as parameters for speculation, is further compounded since I propose to simplify the task by focusing attention on what seem to be the two most important aspects of developments in the United States over the next decades, namely, the availability of resources and the mood of the public as determinants of public policy.

To see things in perspective it is useful to remember that the performance of American society in terms of both economic growth and full employment—the two overriding concerns in the early 1960s—has been impressive. The growth rate of the gross national product increased from 2.4 per cent per year over the period 1953 to 1960 to 6.5 per cent per year over the period 1961 to 1967. Unemployment fell from 7 per cent of the labour force in 1960 to less than 4 per cent in 1968.[27] According to the statistical income standards applied by the Federal government, 22.1 per cent of the population of the United States were considered poor in 1959. Eight years later this figure had shrunk to 13.3 per cent. Yet in spite of this remarkable performance, poverty and economic equality constituted at the end of the 1960s ' more acute and divisive social problems than they had been for a generation, more compelling than at any time in this century save the depths of the Great Depression '.[28] This discrepancy between aspirations and performance is likely to remain a determining factor of American foreign and domestic policy. Unless a major breakdown occurs in the American productive apparatus as a result of racial strife and continued polarization between the affluent and the underprivileged sectors of the population—in the perspective of 1969 not very likely, yet not to be excluded as a future contingency—it would seem reasonable to assume a continued growth of over-all American economic resources at an exponential rate. In the words of a former US Budget Director, ' the United States, already the wealthiest nation in the world, adds the equivalent of a West Germany to its economic base every five years '.[29] If to this one adds the unrivalled American effort in research and development, it seems obvious that the preponderance of the United States in terms of sheer economic, scientific, and technological power is likely to increase sharply over the next decade.

What moods and outlooks will be engendered among the attentive public and among the policy-making and resource-allocating élites in the United States by these pressures and trends? Such a question clearly opens up a wide field for speculation. There are those who argue that the rapid expansion of the material power base in the United States will make American primacy the central feature of world politics.[30] Others see ' a spiritual void, an almost metaphysical boredom with a political environment that increasingly emphasizes bureaucratic challenges and is dedicated to no deeper purpose than material comfort '.[31] The restlessness and dissatisfaction, so conspicuous in American life today, have been centred on the war in Vietnam. But their causes would seem to be more fundamental and to be related rather to basic characteristics of modern technological society than to issues of the moment.[32]

These observations may suggest the following factors as general parameters for the performance of the United States in the world arena during the coming decade: a continued increase in preoccupation with ' the quality of American life ' and thus with domestic rather than foreign policy issues; as a corollary to this and a legacy of Vietnam, a greater reluctance to risk new overseas involvements and a ' tougher ' attitude to the many commitments which will remain; the re-emergence of a longing for new directions and a readiness for ' a new burst of creativity '.[33]

What has been said about the United States is to a certain extent applicable to the more advanced societies in Europe. The predominance of socio-economic and technological issues has been conspicuous in the politics of most West European countries. This trend is likely to persist. To a point, it will continue to favour the pooling of economic and technological resources in order to create an environment in which advanced industries requiring large capital investments and specialized know-how can thrive. But the extent to which these imperatives will guide the future of West European politics depends on so many unpredictable variables that the outcome is uncertain. Since the specific nature of the future configuration will be a crucial determinant for the future role of Western Europe in international affairs, any prediction on that score will have to await firmer indications of the sort of structure that emerges. At present it would seem that Western Europe is entering a period which will no longer be dominated by grand schemes and institutional innovations, but rather by the quest for efficiency, functional co-operation, and *ad hoc* associations for specific purposes. This may eventually lead to an all-European ' system ' of ' overlapping groupings and cross-cutting alignments '. It would not necessarily end the life of the major existing institutions (such as NATO, EEC, WTO, and COMECON), most of which have acquired strong vested interests in self-perpetuation. Nor would it destroy the identity of individual nation-states. Although the ' system ' is likely to be centred around the co-operation of the highly industrialized states in Western Europe, it would be sufficiently flexible and open-ended to permit, and indeed encourage, collaboration or association with the states of Eastern Europe and with certain extra-European countries, such as Canada or Japan.[34]

In the case of the USSR, finally, the central feature of the domestic situation appears to be the contest between two trends: the desire to preserve ideological purity and the leading role of the party bureaucracy as against the need to promote a more pragmatic approach to the central problems of economic development and modernization. The Soviet leadership is faced with the fundamental question of how to adapt a political system built on bureaucratic centralism to the requirements of an advanced industrial society. Recent developments suggest that the present rulers in Moscow are unwilling to face up to this crucial issue, because they see no 'solution' that would not involve *some* abdication of central control. Thus, there is an uneasy parallelism of cautious and distinctly limited modernization of the productive apparatus on the one hand, and an all-pervasive trend towards disciplinarianism and repression on the other. The two are basically incompatible and at some point the leadership must choose between them or yield to those who will.[35] It may be possible for the men in the Kremlin to put off making this decision if they use a rise in tension to rally support. The party leaders have pleaded the dangers of the international situation before in order to stifle political disagreement at home, and it is conceivable that the Brezhnev–Kosygin regime or its successor might use this device again to give the party and the nation a sense of purpose that would cancel the effects of the present quandary. Thus, in the case of the Soviet Union, because of the balance of political forces as they are now, 'the direction of policy may depend primarily on external circumstances'.[36]

The expectations outlined above can hardly provide the basis for an affirmative answer to the question of whether there is a framework for East–West reconciliation in Europe. Yet it can be maintained that they suggest some scope for a potential accommodation. If that is true, we cannot afford to let these possibilities remain unexplored. One approach would be to ask the following questions:

1. What are the basic characteristics of a situation in Europe that could truly be called a 'stable peace'?

2. What procedures could bring about conditions of this kind?

3. How do these substantive and procedural requirements relate to the interests of the main actors and the general expectations postulated in our brief review?

An implicit assumption of the present study has been that the chief problems of peace in Europe are the unresolved Central European issues and the future of East–West relations—that is, that the problems are international in character. But unless the threat of war is seen as imminent, which even during the Czechoslovak crisis of 1968 was not the case, this order of priorities will not be shared by those European nations, particularly in the southern part of the continent, for whom

East–West relations have been of secondary importance. To those nations, the absence of international armed conflict—and even a Central European settlement—will be an insufficient criterion for conditions that would deserve to be called peaceful. So long as social injustice and economic inequality prevail, the concept of peace in Europe will have distinctly different associations for them. This is a reminder to us that peace implies more than the prevention of war, that its domain is not limited to relations between states, but embraces relations between all men. Peace ultimately entails conditions in which the absence of inter-group violence is the reflection of something unquestionably positive: the voluntary, fruitful co-operation of all members in a given society for the common good.

Unfortunately, peace in Europe in this wider sense is not considered as a very pressing problem by the leading powers in Europe, whereas the Central European problems obviously are. The goal must therefore be to find remedies to the latter that will have the capacity to promote solutions of these broader questions.

Peace in Europe in the narrower sense would seem to require, as a minimum, that preoccupations and interests common to rulers and peoples in both East and West override traditional conflicts and differences. The whole European continent must be viewed by the main actors as a ' security-community ' in the sense that the use or threat of force to impose specific solutions would be unthinkable.[37] This situation would imply that no ruling élite or significant pressure group should have a vested interest in exploiting intra-European divisions but on the contrary that it should reasonably expect to reap political benefit from the growth of East–West co-operation in Europe. The processes by which such conditions could be brought about would in principle have to include one or both of the following operations: (1) mutual adaptation of incompatible declared policy objectives, eventually leading to a genuine reconciliation of basic interests; (2) evolution of joint East–West action programmes and co-operative schemes for common purposes sufficiently important to all involved to overshadow conflicting policy goals.

In view of the seemingly intractable nature of the Central European issues, it can be argued that the best hope for an ultimate settlement in Europe still lies in the creation of a pan-European environment of interdependence encompassing in the first instance cultural, technological, and economic co-operation, an environment in which national boundaries would lose some of their present significance and closer contacts eliminate residual fears and suspicions. According to this view, an appropriate strategy for peace in Europe would be one that facilitated functional co-operation across political and ideological boundaries and encouraged overlapping combinations, and which therefore minimized the significance of the dividing line running through Europe. At the same time this strategy would not press for ' solutions ' or formal agreements but would rather encourage the unhampered functioning of trans-national forces of change which in the long run could be expected to operate in favour of a convergence of enlightened self-interest.[38]

This line of argument raises several difficulties. First of all, it is obvious that the general philosophy of the approach outlined above is very similar to that underlying both the American effort at ' peaceful engagement ' in Eastern Europe and the new West German *Ostpolitik*. The implementation of these policies suffered from certain short-comings which we have discussed above and which could be remedied. But one could also challenge the assumption that by pursuing the policies advocated here the West is bound in the long run to bring about a more conciliatory outlook in Moscow based on a greater appreciation of the interests it shares with the West. How long is the long run, and furthermore, is there sufficient ground for confidence that, in the long run, both East and West will see their interests as converging? [39] To these questions there are no obvious answers.

With regard to the time perspective for a possible change in Soviet postures, a conservative estimate appears to be justified. There is no assurance that major modifications in Soviet policy relating to East–West relations will occur in the foreseeable future as a result of events abroad or economic constraints and pressures at home. A 'changing of the guard ' is probably impending in Moscow before very long,[40] if only because of the age of most Soviet officials in key positions.   But one should not underrate the option that is available to any Soviet leadership to muddle through without major shifts in policy—by a combination of measures including some repression, some continued or increased self-isolation, and a certain amount of conscious mismanagement of the economy (which, in a large-scale economy like that of the USSR, need not produce catastrophic results).   As for foreign relations, neither the conflict with China nor the limited community of interests with the United States will necessarily result in a major reorientation of Moscow's European policy.

The role of China in world politics has been of constantly growing concern to the Soviet leadership during the 1960s. By the end of the decade Moscow appeared to view Peking as a major contender, yet in terms of military capabilities, China hardly posed an objective threat to the security of the USSR, nor is it likely to do so in the near future.   There is therefore no reason to expect that the Soviet Union will rush into a European settlement simply to secure its western flank; but it will be in its interest to keep tensions in Europe low enough to enable it to move troops to the eastern border.   The interests that Moscow shares with Washington in avoiding a nuclear conflagration are of such paramount importance to both that neither can exploit this limited community of interests to promote its preferred constellation in Europe.   The only way in which the West can induce Moscow to negotiate a settlement in Europe in a spirit of compromise is to confront the Soviet leadership with the choice between continuing to exploit *détente* for divisive purposes, and using the relaxation of tension as a preliminary to closer co-operation and a preparation for genuine accommodation in Europe.   This would seem to provide the strongest possible incentive for a properly orchestrated long-term approach towards Moscow by the Western allies.

Similarly, one can question the validity of the contention that the enlightened self-interest of ruling élites in East and West will ultimately converge.   We have little reason to assume that greater similarity in the patterns of material production

and consumption in East and West, for which there is some
evidence, will outweigh differences in outlook that are due to
divergences in traditional values and historical experience.[41]
Even an expansion of functional co-operation in Europe across
the East–West dividing line will not by itself give rise to like
hierarchies of values; West European experience in this field
so far gives no reason for optimism on this point.

It seems clear that in addition to the short- and medium-
term measures which I have suggested for stabilizing conditions
in Europe, and in addition to the effects of the ' invisible hand '
of transnational forces in the realm of economic, scientific, and
technological co-operation, something more is required. The
more advanced societies will have to make a concerted effort
to identify areas of common concern that are suitable for joint
action programmes, and to make the ruling élites aware of the
need to accord these questions high priority in practical politics.

Several international issues come to mind, primarily related
to the control of conflict and nuclear armaments, where a
limited yet distinct community of interests has begun to
emerge, at least between the United States and the Soviet
Union. While this is all to the good, since large-scale war
becomes less likely thereby, these problems would hardly seem
to qualify on closer examination for the kind of programmes
meant here, for they do not provide a basis for positive actions
with the potential to make traditional conflicts less and less
important. Issues which could satisfy these requirements would
have to be formulated in more philosphical terms, less attuned
to the current preoccupations of leading politicians. Their
urgency is sensed today only by an attentive but growing
minority, and they do not lend themselves to the kind of
rhetoric that yields immediate political capital. Yet there is
reason to believe that these questions are going to be a source
of growing anxiety for an increasing number of people in
advanced societies. These concerns could be subsumed under
the following broad headings: (1) the protection, preservation,
and improvement of man's physical environment; and (2) the
protection and enrichment of man's human environment.

Under the first point would fall all actions designed to make
the ecological environment of present and future generations

of this planet conducive to a healthy and enjoyable life. This would involve measures to prevent the use of nuclear weapons and other means of mass destruction as a first priority. It would further include massive programmes to raise the standard of living in the Third World. But it would also embrace effective steps more immediately directed towards the solution of the numerous environmental problems besetting the highly industrialized societies, such as air and water pollution, urbanization, the use of pesticides, and so on. The second point would entail common approaches to the responsible use of technical and scientific resources, especially modern means of mass communications, in order to prevent the manipulation of the minds of men and to promote the regeneration of basic human qualities and feelings, such as charity and compassion.[42] This may very well sound like the listing of just so many lofty and pious wishes, somewhat inadvertently appended to an analysis based on empirical data about recent East–West relations. Yet it is this very analysis that has led us to identify these potential areas of common concern between East and West.

Is any one of the problems mentioned above likely to stand out with such an obvious claim to priority that co-operation among the advanced countries would appear self-evident? We cannot exclude such a development as the result of, for example, mass starvation in the Third World or the use of nuclear weapons. But even that cannot be taken for granted, nor can mankind afford to wait so long. Thus a conscious effort to bring the current or potential community of interests of the advanced countries to the attention of political élites and their supporters is an urgent task to be begun today.

This is not the place to speculate about actual procedures that ought to be adopted for this purpose, but it should be emphasized that those who are responsible for giving these issues political relevance are those who understand their implications. The measures to be adopted will depend upon the particular nature of the political system in each country, yet the ultimate task is the same everywhere: to make the ruling élites realize the full importance of these issues. This may appear a Herculean endeavour, but there is evidence in both East and West of an intellectual and emotional readiness, by no means limited to the younger generation, to support political action programmes which have a wider frame of reference than that reflected in the slogans of established politicians.   What is more, this support seems to rest on a common denominator: a deep concern for the whole of humanity and for the conditions of the individual in the age of science and technology.[43]

NOTES

Abbreviations

Bulletin   *Bulletin des Presse- und Informationsamtes der Bundesregierung*
CDSP   *The Current Digest of the Soviet Press*
DOSB   *The Department of State Bulletin*
GAOR   UN, *General Assembly Official Records*
ND   *Notes et études documentaires*, la documentation française
Speeches   *Speeches and Press Conferences*, New York, French Embassy

Introduction

[1] For a discussion of the relationship between the Soviet-American *détente* and the European *détente* see Philip Windsor, ' NATO and European *Détente* ', *The World Today*, 23/9 (1967), pp. 361–9.

[2] Richard Löwenthal convincingly argued that Bonn's new Eastern policy was ' merely the catalyst for a change in Moscow's European policy that corresponded to a general tendency then gaining ground within the Soviet leadership —a tendency towards an increasingly rigid disciplinarianism born of a sense of insecurity that had domestic rather than foreign roots '. ' The Sparrow in the Cage ', *Problems of Communism*, 17/6 (1968), p. 8. See also below, pp. 79 ff.

[3] cf. Thomas C. Schelling, *Arms and Influence* (1966), pp. 264 and 273.

Chapter 1

[1] La documentation française, *Articles et Documents*, 0.1645 (1965), ' Textes du Jour ', p. 5 : English translation from *Speeches*, no. 216.

[2] Ibid. p. 6.

[3] An official statement immediately after the President's press conference of 4 Feb. 1965 emphasized that France maintained the position it had held since the post-war negotiations—that the four former occupying powers were ultimately responsible for the reunification of Germany; *Le Monde*, 6 Feb. 1965. Similarly, in a television interview on 28 Mar. 1966 Prime Minister Pompidou pointed out that a peace treaty between Germany and her former enemies would be the final stage of Germany's reunification, but that this must be preceded by a *détente* in Europe encompassing countries belonging both to NATO and the WTO; *Articles et Documents*, 0.1795 (1966), pp. 4–7.

[4] See e.g. text of joint Franco-Polish declaration, 12 Sept. 1967, at the end of de Gaulle's visit to Poland, *ND*, 3487–9 (1968), p. 73 : English translation, *Official Statements*, no. 145 (New York, French Embassy). Cf. Jacques Vernant, ' Après la conférence de presse 4 février ', *Revue de défense nationale*, 21/4 (1965), pp. 633–8.

[5] *ND*, 3384–7 (1967), pp. 42 f. : *Speeches*, no. 239.

[6] cf. William C. Cromwell, ' The United States ', in W. C. Cromwell, ed., *Political Problems of Atlantic Partnership* (1969), p. 203.

[7] De Gaulle's press conference, 4 Feb. 1965, cited in n. 1 ; cf. Vernant, p. 635. On the border question see also de Gaulle's press conference, 25 Mar. 1959, *L'année politique 1959* (Paris, 1960), p. 616.

[8] See André Passeron, *De Gaulle Parle 1962–1966* (1966), pp. 215 f.

[9] *ND*, 3384–7 (1967), p. 191: *Speeches*, no. 254.

[10] *ND*, 3384–7 (1967), p. 242: *Speeches*, no. 255.

[11] See e.g. his address at the Kremlin, 20 June 1966, *ND*, 3384–7 (1967), p. 103: *Speeches*, no. 247.

[12] See e.g. his press conference of 9 Sept. 1965, Passeron, p. 189, and his Kremlin address, 20 June 1966, cited in n. 11.

[13] This idea expressed by Foreign Minister Couve de Murville in his address to the UN General Assembly, 28 Sept. 1966, *ND*, 3384–7 (1967), p. 147: *Speeches*, no. 252.

[14] See ibid. and de Gaulle's message of 31 Dec. 1966, cited in n. 10.

[15] The inherent inconsistencies in France's Eastern policy became more visible during de Gaulle's state visit to Poland in Sept. 1967. His compartmentalization of Europe into Eastern, Central, and Western regions, implying a differentiation between Polish and Soviet policy, was met by Gomulka's rejoinder that the basic principle of Poland's foreign policy was maintenance of the alliance with the USSR and co-operation with other socialist countries in Europe. See speeches of de Gaulle and Gomulka to the Polish parliament, 11 Sept. 1967, *Europa-Archiv*, 22/19 (1967), pp. D447 f. and D448–51, resp.

[16] To the National Assembly, 3 Nov. 1966, Couve de Murville stated that 'the over-all situation in Europe lends itself to long-range views and allows us to study a long-term policy, for the time of adventures seems past there now. This situation has indeed stabilized enough for us to feel that, in the present state, external events alone could challenge it.' *ND*, 3384–7 (1967), p. 192: *Speeches*, no. 254.

[17] cf. U. Kitzinger, *The Politics and Economics of European Integration* (1963), pp. 140 ff., and R. N. Rosecrance, *Defense of the Realm* (1968), pp. 255 ff.

[18] See e.g. House of Commons speeches by Prime Minister Wilson, 8 May 1967, and Mr Heath, 9 May 1967, HC Deb., vol. 746, coll. 1094 f. and 1296, resp.

[19] See below, pp. 39 f.

[20] For an analysis of earlier, more daring policy positions adopted by Britain which tended to embroil her with Bonn *and* Paris, see S. Hoffmann, *Gulliver's Troubles* (1968), p. 440.

[21] Concerning the indirect British recognition of the Oder-Neisse line as the final border between Germany and Poland, see Foreign Secretary Brown's comment on the UK-USSR communiqué issued after Kosygin's visit to Britain in Feb. 1967, *The Times*, 15 Feb. 1967; also statement of Goronwy Roberts, minister of state for foreign affairs, to the House of Commons, 31 May 1968, HC Deb., vol. 765, coll. 2354 ff. This position was shared not only by France but at least implicitly by all Western governments.

[22] See statement of Britain's minister of state for foreign affairs, Lord Chalfont, to the WEU Assembly on 17 June 1966, Assembly of Western European Union, *Proceedings, 12th ordy sess., 1st part, vol. II, Minutes and Official Report of Debates* (Paris, 1966), p. 230.

[23] HC Deb., vol. 742, col. 289.

[24] Ibid. coll. 110 f.

[25] *Statement on the Defence Estimates 1967* (London, HMSO, Cmnd. 3203, 1967), p. 4. According to press reports, Denis Healey argued forcefully at the closed ministerial meeting of the NATO Council in Paris, Dec. 1966, that the improvement in East–West relations was fundamental and lasting. His US colleague allegedly expressed far greater scepticism and cautioned the West European allies against assuming basic changes in Soviet policy. See Henry Tanner's report from Paris, *The New York Times*, 15 Dec. 1966.

[26] See e.g. Chalfont's statement to the WEU Assembly, 17 June 1966, cited in n. 22, and his article, ' Value of Observation Posts in NATO and Warsaw Pact Areas ', *European Review*, 16/4 (1966), pp. 31–3.

[27] See e.g. speech of Foreign Secretary Brown, at the International Publishing Corpn Conference of European Editors, London, 21 Nov. 1966, partly reprinted as ' East–West Relations and the European Problem ', *NATO Letter*, 15/2 (1967), pp. 2–5.

[28] See Edward Heath's speech, 9 May 1967, HC Deb., vol. 746, col. 1296.

[29] Speech in Paris, 19 July 1966, *DOSB*, 55/1419 (1966), p. 343.

[30] Ibid. p. 342.

[31] Speech at New York, 21 Apr. 1967, *DOSB*, 56/1455 (1967), p. 753.

[32] Speech at Luxembourg, 11 Sept. 1967, *DOSB*, 57/1475 (1967), p. 425.

[33] See above, p. 13.

[34] William C. Foster, ' New Directions in Arms Control and Disarmament ', *Foreign Affairs*, 43/4 (1964/5), p. 600.

[35] See his statement, 30 June 1966, US Senate, Cttee on Foreign Relations, *United States Policy Toward Europe (and Related Matters)*, Hearings, 89th Cong., 2nd sess., pp. 311 f.; also his *The Discipline of Power* (1968), pp. 287 ff.

[36] US House of Repres, Cttee on Foreign Affs, Subcttee on Europe, *The Crisis in NATO*, Hearings, 89th Cong., 2nd sess., pp. 71 ff.

[37] US Senate, Cttee on Foreign Relations, *United States Policy Toward Europe (and Related Matters)*, Hearings, 89th Cong., 2nd sess., p. 161.

[38] See e.g. President Johnson's New York speech, 7 Oct. 1966, *DOSB*, 55/1426 (1966), pp. 622–5; and Vice-President Humphrey's New York speech, 23 May 1968, *DOSB*, 58/1512 (1968), pp. 793–7.

[39] cf. Z. Brzezinski, *Alternative to Partition* (1965), pp. 117 ff., and John C. Campbell, *American Policy Toward Eastern Europe* (1965), pp. 87 ff.

[40] See his remarks at Lexington, Va., 23 May 1964, *DOSB*, 50/1303 (1964), p. 923.

[41] See US House of Repres, Cttee on Foreign Affs, Subcttee on Europe, *Recent Developments in the Soviet Bloc*, Hearings, 88th Cong., 2nd sess., part II, pp. 350 ff.

[42] On 25 Feb. 1964 Secretary Rusk emphasized that the US wanted the East European peoples to live ' in friendship with their Russian and other neighbours ' and ' to develop in accordance with their own national aspirations and genius ', *DOSB*, 50/1290 (1964), pp. 390–6.

[43] Robert Byrnes called the new approach ' active or positive containment '. In his view, it was based on the same confident assumption as the original doctrine of containment of 1947, namely, ' that the Soviet position . . . in Eastern Europe . . . will not be permanent '. R. F. Byrnes, ' American Opportunities and Dilemmas ', in R. F. Byrnes, ed., *The United States and Eastern Europe* (1967), p. 159. This was probably true as late as 1964, but it seems that by 1966 the prevailing view in the US administration was that ' peaceful engagement ' must not be presented as a policy designed to sow discord between the USSR and the East European countries. See e.g. Rusk's address at New York, 22 Aug. 1966, *DOSB*, 55/1420 (1966), p. 366.

[44] *DOSB*, 55/1426 (1966), p. 623.

[45] ' Toward a Community of the Developed Nations ' (based on speech at Carleton University, Ottawa, 20 Jan. 1967), *DOSB*, 56/1446 (1967), p. 418.

[46] Brzezinski, *Alternative to Partition*, pp. 139–41.

[47] *DOSB*, 50/1303 (1964), p. 923.

[48] Brzezinski, *Alternative to Partition*, p. 123.

[49] *DOSB*, 55/1426 (1966), p. 623.

[50] Ibid. pp. 623 f.

[51] This linkage was not made much clearer by Brzezinski's exegesis in early 1967, that the ' building of Western unity creates stability in Europe and is therefore in keeping with the thrust of history ', and that ' East–West policies must be compatible with this thrust if they are to resolve the European problem '. ' Toward a Community of the Developed Nations ', *DOSB*, 56/1446 (1967), p. 418.

[52] See the address of Harlan Cleveland, 19 July 1966, *DOSB*, 55/1419 (1966), p. 343; of President Johnson, 7 Oct. 1966, cited in n. 49; and of Under Secretary Rostow at San Francisco, 3 May 1968, *DOSB*, 58/1509 (1968), pp. 680–6.

[53] For US insistence on co-ordinated approaches towards the East, see President Johnson's address of 7 Oct. 1966, cited in n. 49, and Vice-President Humphrey's address in Washington, 21 Apr. 1967, quoted in Cromwell, p. 206.

[54] Secretary Rusk's address, 25 Feb. 1964, *DOSB*, 50/1290 (1964), pp. 390–6.

[55] See report of debate on the 1966 Agricultural Appropriation Act, *The New York Times*, 13 Dec. 1966. An example of this lack of receptiveness was Congressman Paul A. Fino's statement that ' frankly, . . . I am out to burn the bloody bridges the President is building to the East; I think that they are short on economic and political plausibility and long on naivety '. *Congressional Record*, 10 Apr. 1967, p. H3790.

[56] cf. Z. Brzezinski, ' The Framework of East–West Reconciliation ', *Foreign Affairs*, 46/2 (1967/8), pp. 256–75. The author points out the difficulty of reconciling the original concept of Atlantic partnership with the new vision of a Europe made whole.

[57] cf. Arnulf Baring, *Aussenpolitik in Adenauers Kanzlerdemokratie* (1969), pp. 61 f., 138 ff.; also Immanuel Birnbaum, *Entzweite Nachbarn* (1968), pp. 156 ff.

[58] *Keesing's Archiv der Gegenwart* (1955), p. 5514.

[59] See e.g. the speech delivered by the Minister for Refugees and Expellees, J. B. Gradl, 28 Nov. 1965, *Bulletin*, 187 (1965), p. 1512.

[60] In a first effort to adapt its position to the prevailing Western stand, West Germany issued a ' Peace Note ' on 25 Mar. 1966, *Europa-Archiv*, 21/7 (1966), pp. D171–5. It upheld the basic linkage between *détente* and steps towards reunification even though it was more conciliatory in tone than previous statements.

[61] See e.g. the statements of Kai-Uwe von Hassel in autumn 1964 when he was minister of defence, reprinted in his *Verantwortung für die Freiheit* (1965), pp. 92 ff. and 126 ff.

[62] In an analysis of *détente* the West German politician Carlo Schmidt distinguished between tensions due to fear of losing a vital possession and those due to fear of being frustrated in a basic aspiration to which one feels entitled. See his speech to the Council of Europe, 27 Sept. 1966, partly reprinted in *Europa-Archiv*, 21/24 (1966), pp. D 636–41.

[63] See his speech, 3 June 1966, *Arbeitsgemeinschaft B, Tatsachen-Argumente Nr. 205/66*, *SPD Parteitag 1966* (Bonn, Vorstand der SPD, 1966), pp. 4 f.

[64] cf. Philip Shabecoff, ' Indignation in Bonn ', *New York Times*, 18 Oct. 1966.

[65] For detailed account of events leading to the formation of the Grand Coalition, see e.g. Michael Balfour, *West Germany* (1968), pp. 250 ff.

[66] *Europa-Archiv*, 22/1 (1967), p. D15.

[67] Brandt's speech to the Council of Europe, 24 Jan. 1967, *Europa-Archiv*, 22/4 (1967), pp. D81 f.

[68] ' *Détente* over the Long Haul ', *Survival*, 9/10 (1967), p. 312, originally ' Entspannungspolitik mit langem Atem ', *Aussenpolitik*, 18/8 (1967), pp. 449–54.

[69] Ibid. and Brandt's speech of 24 Jan. 1967.

[70] See interview with Brandt, 11 Aug. 1967, *Bulletin*, 87 (1967), pp. 745 ff.

[71] See Willy Brandt, *Aussenpolitik, Deutschlandpolitik, Europapolitik* (1968), pp. 86 ff., his interview in *Moderne Welt*, 8/4 (1967), pp. 358 ff., and his ' German Policy Towards the East ', *Foreign Affairs*, 46/3 (1967/8), pp. 476–86.

[72] Sometimes a third possibility was mentioned in the West German debate, namely that a system overarching the alliances without disposing of them might be created. See Erhard Eppler, ' Die europäische Funktion der Deutschen ', *Die Zeit*, 27 Oct. 1967, reprinted in his *Spannungsfelder* (1968).

[73] Interview, *Moderne Welt*, 8/4 (1967), p. 358.

[74] See W. Brandt, *Survival*, 9/10 (1967), p. 312, and his *Friedenspolitik in Europa* (1968), p. 189. Kiesinger expressed a similar view in a speech to the Deutsche Gesellschaft für Auswärtige Politik, 23 June 1967, summarized in *Europa-Archiv*, 22/18 (1967), pp. 683 f.

[75] Interviews, 24 Apr. and 2 July 1967, and speech in Düsseldorf, 30 Nov. 1967, W. Brandt, *Aussenpolitik, Deutschlandpolitik, Europapolitik*, pp. 56, 86, 156, resp.

[76] W. Brandt, *Foreign Affairs*, 46/3 (1967/8), pp. 477 f. His assertion was clearly meant to refute the earlier article by Brzezinski in *Foreign Affairs*, 46/2 (1967/8), in which ' the end of the Atlantic orientation in Bonn ' was announced. See also W. Brandt, *Friedenspolitik*, pp. 159 ff.

[77] Interview, *Moderne Welt*, 8/4 (1967), pp. 358, 359, 361. See also the government declaration, 13 Oct. 1967, reprinted in W. Brandt, *Aussenpolitik, Deutschlandpolitik, Europapolitik*, p. 129.

[78] We disregard here statements made during the election campaign of 1969, which led to a polarization of views implying in the case of Kiesinger a return to some of the positions held by the CDU prior to Dec. 1966.

[79] See Kiesinger's address to the Deutsche Gesellschaft für Auswärtige Politik, 23 June 1967. There he spoke of the ' critical size ' of a united Germany which could not be accommodated in the existing European structure without causing major imbalances and expressed himself in favour of a *détente* between the alliances leading eventually to co-operation between them. See also his press conference in Washington, 16 Aug. 1967, *Europa-Archiv*, 22/18 (1967), p. D419. For Brandt's views see above, p. 32.

[80] See Kiesinger's addresses of 9 Mar. 1967, 11 Mar. 1968, and 24 Dec. 1968, and his radio interview of 25 Aug. 1968: *Bulletin*, 26 (1967), p. 206; 33 (1968), p. 263; 104 (1968), p. 889; and 165 (1968), pp. 1445–6, resp.

[81] cf. W. Brandt, *Aussenpolitik, Deutschlandpolitik, Europapolitik*, pp. 146 and 158.

[82] cf. Kiesinger's address, 9 Mar. 1967, as in n. 80.

[83] See Kiesinger's speeches of 11 Mar. and 24 Dec. 1968, as in n. 80, and 11 Apr. 1969, *Bulletin*, 46 (1969), p. 391.

[84] The subtitle of his book *Herausforderung und Antwort* (1968).

[85] W. Brandt, *Friedenspolitik*, pp. 77 ff. and 90.

[86] Strauss, *The Grand Design* (1966), p. 18.

[87] He envisaged the forming of a *Zwischeneuropa* (literally, an in-between, or intermediate, Europe) controlled neither by Moscow nor by the West Europeans. Strauss, *Herausforderung und Antwort*, p. 147.

[88] Ibid. pp. 111 f.

[89] In Strauss's scheme the new Europe would be ' associated with the United States, but not under its military control '. Ibid. p. 148.

[90] Ibid. p. 147.

[91] Memoranda between the USSR and West Germany, *Europa-Archiv*, 23/16 (1968), pp. D361–86.

[92] Due to Soviet counter-measures, the success of this West German initiative

was limited to the establishment of diplomatic relations with Rumania in early 1967, the exchange of trade missions with Czechoslovakia in Aug. 1967, and the resumption of diplomatic relations with Yugoslavia in Jan. 1968. See below, pp. 60 ff.

93 See the government declaration, 13 Dec. 1966, *Europa-Archiv,* 22/1 (1967), p. D18; also Brandt's speech to the Council of Europe, 24 Jan. 1967, in which he used the term ' orderly coexistence ' (' *Geregeltes Nebeneinander* ') to describe the relation Bonn was seeking to attain with East Berlin, *Europa-Archiv,* 22/4 (1967), p. D84.

94 W. Brandt, *Survival,* 9/10 (1967), p. 311.

95 His speech, 24 Jan. 1967, *Europa-Archiv,* 22/4 (1967), p. D85.

96 cf. Marshall D. Shulman, ' " Europe " versus " *Détente* " ? ', *Foreign Affairs,* 45/3 (1966/7), pp. 391 f.

97 This preference induced Harlan Cleveland to twist the original meaning of *détente* to the point where he argued that ' a modern Clausewitz might . . . translate *détente* as a " continuation of tension by other means " '. *DOSB,* 58/1509 (1968), p. 690.

98 cf. Brzezinski ' Toward a Community of the Developed Nations ', *DOSB,* 56/1446 (1967), pp. 414–20.

99 See e.g. Rusk's address at Chicago, 6 July 1967, *DOSB,* 57/1465 (1967), p. 90; for McNamara's views early in 1967 see *Statement of Secretary of Defense Robert S. McNamara before the House Armed Services Committee on the Fiscal Year 1968–72 Defense Program and 1968 Defense Budget* (1967), p. 24. NATO's Scandinavian members backed this position strongly; see K. E. Birnbaum, ' The Nordic Countries and European Security ', *Co-operation and Conflict,* 3/1 (1968), pp. 9 f.

100 Kiesinger's speech, 9 Mar. 1967, reflected the problem clearly: ' We do not say first reunification, then *détente.* Nor do we say first *détente,* then reunification. We say : *détente* and in this process of *détente* the problem of German reunification must never for a moment be lost sight of—either by ourselves or by the others.' *Bulletin,* 26 (1967), p. 206, author's translation.

101 cf. Karl Kaiser, ' Deutsche Aussenpolitik nach der tschechoslowakischen Krise von 1968 ', *Europa-Archiv,* 24/10 (1969), p. 363.

102 cf. Hoffman, p. 429.

103 cf. Uwe Nerlich, *Europäische Sicherheit der 70er Jahre* (1968), p. 24; Hans Kuby, ' German Foreign, Defence, and European Policy ', *Journal of Common Market Studies,* 6/2 (1967/8), pp. 156 ff.

104 Annex to final communiqué of NATO Council meeting in Luxembourg, 12–14 Dec. 1967, ' Future Tasks of the Alliance ', *DOSB,* 58/1489 (1968), pp. 50–2, esp. paras. 7–13.

105 For discussion of different ' visions ' within the Atlantic alliance, bi-polar *v.* multi-polar, and Atlantic *v.* European, cf. Hoffman, p. 407 ff.

106 Attachment to communiqué issued after the ministerial session of NATO Council at Reykjavik, 24 and 25 June 1968, ' Mutual and Balanced Force Reductions ', *DOSB,* 59/1516 (1968), p. 77. France associated herself only with those paragraphs which did not conflict with her right to control her own national forces. But Paris could hardly object to measures which, if implemented, would have decreased the military potential of the two superpowers in the heart of Europe.

Chapter 2

1 This section is to a large extent based on the following works: J. F. Brown, *The New Eastern Europe* (1966), Alexander Dallin and Thomas B. Larson, eds.,

Soviet Politics Since Khrushchev (1968), and Michael Gamarnikow, 'Political Patterns and Economic Reforms ', *Problems of Communism*, 18/2 (1969), pp. 11–23.

² This point was made by the Hungarian government's scientific adviser on economic policy, Professor József Bognár, in a lecture at the Swedish Institute of International Affairs, 25 Apr. 1967.

³ cf. Marshall D. Shulman, 'Recent Soviet Foreign Policy ', *Journal of International Affairs*, 22/1 (1968), pp. 26–47. For a Soviet assessment contemporary to the Congress, see D. Tomashevsky, 'The USSR and the Capitalist World ', *International Affairs* (Moscow), 13/3 (1966), pp. 13–17.

⁴ My italics. Report of CPSU Central Committee to 23rd Congress of the CPSU delivered by the First Secretary of the Central Cttee, Leonid I. Brezhnev, 29 Mar. 1966, *Pravda*, 30 Mar. 1966: *CDSP*, 18/12 (1966), p. 5.

⁵ Ibid. See also speeches, 2 Apr. 1966, of Andrei A. Gromyko, USSR minister of foreign affairs, and R. Malinovsky, USSR minister of defence, to 23rd Party Congress where Malinovsky spoke of ' the complex nature of the international situation and the increasing military provocations of the imperialist powers ', *Pravda*, 3 Apr. 1966: *CDSP*, 18/17 (1966), pp. 16–19 and 11–13, resp.

⁶ cf. Tomashevsky, and see e.g. Gromyko's speech, 2 Apr. 1966.

⁷ See Gromyko's comments on Brezhnev's report in his speech of 2 Apr. 1966. In the report itself this requirement was stressed even more: ' The CPSU Central Committee sets forth for the future . . . *as one of the principal directions of the foreign-policy activity of the Party and the Soviet state the development and consolidation of ideological and political ties with the Communist Parties of all the countries of socialism . . . the development and consolidation of the USSR's political, economic, and other ties with socialist states, the promotion in every way possible of the solidarity of the socialist commonwealth, and the strengthening of its might and influence.*' Italics in the original, *Pravda*, 30 Mar. 1966: *CDSP*, 18/12 (1966), pp. 6 f.

⁸ Ibid.; cf. Tomashevsky.

⁹ Speech of 2 Apr. 1966, cited in n. 5.

¹⁰ *Pravda*, 30 Sept. 1965, as quoted in Malcolm Mackintosh, ' The Evolution of the Warsaw Pact ', *Adelphi Papers*, 58 (1969), p. 9.

¹¹ Brezhnev's report, 29 Mar. 1966, and Malinovsky's speech, 2 Apr. 1966. Malinovsky emphasized the importance of the expansion of combat co-operation with the armies of the other Warsaw Treaty members, and asserted that the further strengthening of these ' fraternal ties and unity . . . must . . . be an object of our unflagging concern '.

¹² Speech on 45th anniversary of the Rumanian CP, 7 May 1966, published under the title *The Romanian Communist Party—Continuer of the Romanian People's Revolutionary and Democratic Struggle, of the Working-Class and Socialist Movement in Romania* (Bucharest, Agerpres, 1966), pp. 97 f.

¹³ At Pitesti, 11 June 1966, *Documents, Articles and Information on Romania* (Bucharest, Agerpres), 17/11 (1966), pp. 12 f.

¹⁴ Speech of 7 May 1966, cited in n. 12, pp. 98 f.

¹⁵ For account of this dialogue, see Gerhard Wettig, ' Die europäische Sicherheit in der Politik des Ostblocks 1966 ', *Osteuropa*, 17/2–3 (1967), pp. 94–113; also R. A. Remington, ' The Changing Soviet Perception of the Warsaw Pact ', unpublished MS, Nov. 1967, Center for International Studies, MIT, C/67–24.

¹⁶ cf. Gromyko's speech of 2 Apr. 1966, cited in n. 5.

¹⁷ In a later speech at Pulawy, 16 July 1966, the Polish leader, Wladyslaw Gromyko's called the growth of the forces campaigning for the maintenance and consolidation of peace the ' predominating tendency '; but in the Bucharest document itself it was presented as only ' one of the dominant features of the

present international situation '. See the official publication *Polish Viewpoint: Disarmament, Denuclearization, European Security* (Warsaw, Polonia Publishing House, 1967), pp. 62 and 51.

[18] This and all subsequent quotations from the Bucharest Declaration are taken from the official translation published by Agerpres, Bucharest.

[19] cf. Vaclav Kotyk, ' Problems of East-West Relations ', *Journal of International Affairs*, 22/1 (1968), p. 53.

[20] Yury Zhukov, ' Paths of Europe ', *Pravda*, 20 May 1966: *CDSP*, 18/20 (1966), p. 14. See also Gromyko's speech, 2 Apr. 1966, *Pravda*, 3 Apr. 1966: *CDSP*, 18/17 (1966), pp. 17–18.

[21] See *Polish Viewpoint*, p. 48.

[22] For Polish and Czechoslovak interest in having the US participate in discussions on European security, see remarks of the Polish foreign minister, Adam Rapacki, during his visit to Scandinavia, e.g. as reproduced in foreign policy debate of the Swedish *Riksdag*, 8 Mar. 1967, *Riksdagens protokoll, Andra Kammaren*, 12 (1967), and Ladislav Liska, ' On the Problem of European Security ', *International Relations* (Prague), 1967, p. 25. The ambiguity of the Soviet position is evident in Kosygin's replies at his press conference in Paris, 4 Dec. 1966, *Pravda*, 5 Dec. 1966: *CDSP*, 18/49 (1966), pp. 3–6.

[23] cf. Wettig, *Osteuropa*, 17/2–3 (1967), p. 99.

[24] See report of Walter Ulbricht to 13th meeting of the Socialist Unity Party of Germany (SED), 15 Sept. 1966, *Die Deutsche Demokratische Republik, die Europäische Sicherheit und die Entspannung der Beziehungen zwischen beiden deutschen Staaten* (Berlin, Dietz Verlag, 1966).

[25] See speech of Józef Cyrankiewicz, chairman of the council of ministers of the Polish People's Republic, on 27th anniversary of the German attack on Poland, 1 Sept. 1966, *Trybuna Ludu* (Warsaw), 2 Sept. 1966: *Polish Facts and Figures* (London, Polish Embassy), 795 (1966), p. 1.

[26] His speech at Pulawy, 16 July 1966, *Polish Viewpoint*, pp. 62–6.

[27] See three articles (in Russian) by N. Polyanov, R. Fyodorov, and Yu. Bochkaryov, under the rubric ' Problems of International Security ', *Kommunist* (Moscow), 43/11 (1966), pp. 89–122.

[28] Ye. Pralnikov, ' Problems of European Security; Sinister Axis ', *Izvestia*, 16 July 1966: *CDSP*, 18/28 (1966), pp. 14–16.

[29] P. Naumov, ' European Security ', *Pravda*, 21 Sept. 1966: *CDSP*, 18/38 (1966), pp. 26 f.

[30] Speech at the Soviet-Polish friendship rally, 15 Oct. 1966, *Pravda*, 16 Oct. 1966: *CDSP*, 18/42 (1966), pp. 3–5.

[31] A turning point in the East German government's attitude to West Germany was the cancellation of the proposed exchange of speakers between the SPD and the SED. Cf. Gottfried Vetter, ' Zur Entwicklung der innerdeutschen Beziehungen ', *Europa-Archiv*, 23/9 (1968), pp. 309–19.

[32] See Ulbricht's speech to 14th Plenary Session of Central Committee of the SED, 15 Dec. 1966, *Neues Deutschland*, 16 Dec. 1966.

[33] See authorized report by the East German Press Agency (ADN), *Neues Deutschland*, 17 Jan. 1967.

[34] N. Polyanov, ' Judge Bonn's Policy by its Deeds ', *Izvestia*, 16 Dec. 1966: *CDSP*, 18/50 (1967), pp. 18 f. For detailed review and analysis of Soviet attitudes towards Bonn during the first months of the new government, see Gerhard Wettig, ' Moskau und die Grosse Koalition in Bonn ', *Aus Politik und Zeitgeschichte*, supplement to the weekly *Das Parlament*, 10 (1968).

[35] See *Documents, Articles and Information on Romania* (Agerpres), 18/3 (1967), p. 19.

[36] It is probably indicative of the East German leadership's uneasiness in face of the new signals from Bonn that in his New Year message of 31 Dec. 1966 Ulbricht raised several new demands as preconditions for a *détente* in intra-German relations. See *Europa-Archiv*, 22/5 (1967), pp. D102–4.

[37] *Pravda*, 14 Jan. 1967: *CDSP*, 19/2 (1967), pp. 3–5.

[38] Soviet government statement, handed to Western diplomatic representatives on 28 Jan. 1967, *Pravda*, 29 Jan. 1967: *CDSP*, 19/4 (1967), pp. 11–13.

[39] Note of 7 Feb. 1967, *Pravda* and *Izvestia*, 9 Feb. 1967: *CDSP*, 19/6 (1967), pp. 21 f.

[40] Speech to Party conference, Katowice, 7 Feb. 1967: German translation in *Europa-Archiv*, 22/6 (1967), pp. D120–2.

[41] Address to Central Committee of the CPCS, 8 Feb. 1967: German translation in *Europa-Archiv*, 22/6 (1967), pp. D122 f.

[42] See Ulbricht's speech to the Party *Aktiv*, Berlin, 13 Feb. 1967, *Europa-Archiv*, 22/6 (1967), pp. D124–9.

[43] B. Pyadyshev and R. Sergeyev, ' Meeting in Warsaw ', *Pravda*, 24 Feb. 1967: *CDSP*, 19/8 (1967), pp. 16 f.

[44] Speech, 10 Mar. 1967, BBC *Summary of World Broadcasts*, pt 2, 2nd series, EE/2414/A1/2, 13 Mar. 1967.

[45] Press conference in Copenhagen, 6 Mar. 1967, *Neue Zürcher Zeitung*, 8 Mar. 1967.

[46] *Europa-Archiv*, 22/8 (1967), pp. D191–4 and D194–6, resp.

[47] Spartak Beglov, ' A Europe of Inviolable Borders ', *Pravda*, 10 Apr. 1967: *CDSP*, 19/15 (1967), p. 21.

[48] See Brezhnev's speech to 7th Congress of the SED in East Berlin, 18 Apr. 1967, *Pravda*, 19 Apr. 1967: *CDSP*, 19/16 (1967), p. 5.

[49] Speech to voters in a Moscow electoral district, 10 Mar. 1967, *Pravda*, 11 Mar. 1967.

[50] Brezhnev's speech to the Karlovy Vary conference, held 24–26 Apr. 1967, *Information Bulletin* (Prague, Peace and Socialism Publishers), 8 (1967), p. 35.

[51] See the ' Statement by European Communist and Workers' Parties, Participants in the Conference at Karlovy Vary ', ibid. 9/10 (1967), p. 104.

[52] Extracts from his speech at the Karlovy Vary conference, 24 Apr. 1967, *Polish Viewpoint*, p. 74; cf. Wolfgang Berner, ' Die Karlsbader Konferenz der Kommunistischen Parteien Europas ', *Berichte des Bundesinstituts für ostwissenschaftliche und internationale Studien*, 30 (1967), p. 16.

[53] F. Burlatsky, V. Zhuravsky, and V. Nekrasov, ' Concrete Programme of Struggle for the Security of Peoples ', *Pravda*, 26 Apr. 1967: *CDSP*, 19/17 (1967), pp. 11 f.

[54] Ibid.

[55] His speech at Karlovy Vary, as n. 50, pp. 27 and 32; also the joint UK-USSR statement on results of Kosygin's visit to Britain, which emphasized the importance of encouraging bilateral contacts and co-operation among European countries and of creating an atmosphere of trust among all the countries of Eastern and Western Europe. *Pravda*, 14 Feb. 1967; *CDSP*, 19/7 (1967), p. 3.

[56] *Information Bulletin* (Prague), 8 (1967), p. 56.

[57] His report to 8th Plenary Session of Central Committee of the Polish United Workers' Party, *Nowe Drogi*, June 1967, p. 42.

[58] *Information Bulletin* (Prague), 9–10 (1967), p. 54.

[59] Ibid. p. 56.

[60] Speech, ibid., p. 23.

[61] Ibid. p. 105.

[62] The concluding paragraph of the statement runs: ' The European peoples are capable of deciding themselves the question of peace and security on their continent. Let them take the destinies of Europe into their own hands!' Ibid. p. 108.

[63] See above, p. 65.

[64] See Bucharest Declaration of July 1966, cited in n. 18.

[65] *Information Bulletin* (Prague), 9–10 (1967), p. 104.

[66] cf. Adam B. Ulam, *Expansion and Coexistence: The History of Soviet Foreign Policy 1917–1967* (1968), pp. 557 ff.

[67] See Brezhnev's report to 23rd Party Congress, 29 Mar. 1966, *CDSP*, 18/12 (1966), p. 13, and his ' election address ' of 10 Mar. 1967, *Pravda*, 11 Mar. 1966. See also the consistent arguments for a Europe without America advanced by *Pravda*'s editorial writer Yury Zhukov in the issues of 20 May 1966: *CDSP*, 18/20 (1966), p. 14, and 6, 12, 21 Mar. 1968: *CDSP*, 20/12 (1968), pp. 3–6.

[68] Brezhnev's report to 23rd Party Congress, 29 Mar. 1966, cited in n. 4.

[69] *Information Bulletin* (Prague), 8 (1967), p. 32.

[70] Gerhard Kegel, ' Zur Deutschlandpolitik der beiden Deutschlands ', *Einheit*, 28/6 (1968), p. 736.

[71] See Ulbricht's speech of 31 Dec. 1967 in which he emphasized the obligation of the GDR and its citizens to lend ' political and moral ' support to the ' peace-loving and democratic ' forces in West Germany in order to help them eliminate militarism, nazism, and the predominance of monopoly capitalism, *Neues Deutschland*, 1 Jan. 1968.

[72] See e.g. Ceausescu's speech to the Grand National Assembly, 24 July 1967, published under the title *Speech concerning the Foreign Policy of the Communist Party and of the Romanian Government* (Bucharest, Agerpres, 1967), pp. 50–4.

[73] See Ulbricht's speech to the Karlovy Vary conference, *Information Bulletin* (Prague), 9–10 (1967), p. 60.

[74] See statement by Foreign Minister Rapacki to the UN General Assembly, 14 Dec. 1964, *Polish Viewpoint*, p. 35.

[75] Polish government Note, 28 Apr. 1966, to the West German government. Present author's italics. Ibid. p. 45.

[76] From Gomulka's speech, 15 Mar. 1967, when Poland concluded a bilateral friendship treaty with the GDR; ibid. p. 72. Although the Polish leaders did not rule out German reunification, after 1967 recognition of the GDR was not to my knowledge linked with this issue in any official Polish pronouncements.

[77] For the various Polish proposals, see *Polish Viewpoint*, pp. 4–48.

[78] cf. Nerlich, pp. 33 ff.

[79] See Janos Kadar's proposal, June 1966, for a non-aggression pact between NATO and the WTO, *Neues Deutschland*, 16 June 1966; also the resolution of the Hungarian National Assembly, 14 July 1967, *Europa-Archiv*, 22/18 (1967), pp. D421 f.

[80] His speech to the UN General Assembly, 10 Oct. 1967, *GAOR*, 22nd sess., plen. mtg 1584, 10 Oct. 1967.

[81] See speech by Foreign Minister Peter, 14 July 1967, to the Hungarian National Assembly, and the Assembly resolution of same date, *Europa-Archiv*, 22/18 (1967), pp. D420 and 421 f.

Chapter 3

[1] CTK (Prague) press release, 10 Apr. 1968.

[2] For a detailed and suggestive interpretation of Soviet policy leading up to the invasion of Czechoslovakia, see Löwenthal, pp. 2–28.

³ On the significance of ' properly ' assessing the danger arising from West German ' militarism and revanchism ' as a touchstone of socialist solidarity, see above, p. 65.

⁴ See e.g. Dubcek's speech of 22 Feb. 1968, *Rude Pravo*, 23 Feb. 1968: BBC *Summary of World Broadcasts*, pt 2, 2nd series, EE/2704/C/1–8, 24 Feb. 1968.

⁵ See Ota Vaclavik, ' Uroven a moznosti zahranicni politiky ', *Rude Pravo*, 27 Mar. 1968.

⁶ Report by Dubcek at the Plenary Session of the CPCS Central Committee, 1 Apr. 1968. *ND*, 3532 (1968), pp. 42–4.

⁷ See the Action Programme, 5 Apr. 1968, as n. 1.

⁸ Philip Windsor has rightly pointed out that the new leaders in Prague were careful not to change Czechoslovakia's foreign policy, see P. Windsor and Adam Roberts, *Czechoslovakia 1968* (1969), p. 19. Yet these leaders' public attitude to the situation in Europe was very different from Moscow's and could be interpreted as preparation for a policy change, particularly as regards relations with West Germany, the touchstone of WTO solidarity.

⁹ See e.g. Brezhnev's speech to the Moscow party organization, 29 Mar. 1968, *Pravda*, 30 Mar. 1968: *CDSP*, 20/13 (1968), p. 6.

¹⁰ For full text of the resolution, see *Pravda*, 11 Apr. 1968: *CDSP*, 20/15 (1968), pp. 3 f.

¹¹ See the article with this title in *Sovetskaya Rossia*, 13 Apr. 1968: *CDSP*, 20/15 (1968), p. 4.

¹² The letter was signed by some seventy artists, scientists, and workers who expressed concern about the threat of foreign intervention and about the possibility of continuing the process of democratization. They recommended strikes and boycotts in order to force the remaining conservative elements in the party leadership to resign. For English translation, see *The Times Literary Supplement*, 18 July 1968.

¹³ On 11 July 1968, the Soviet government began to publish the documents handed to the West German government during the confidential diplomatic exchanges started early in 1967. The West German authorities immediately reciprocated. All these documents are published in *Europa-Archiv*, 23/16 (1968), pp. D362 ff.

¹⁴ For full text of the ' Warsaw Letter ', see *Pravda*, 18 July 1968: *CDSP*, 20/29 (1968), pp. 4–6.

¹⁵ ' The point of view of the Presidium of the Czechoslovak Communist Party Central Committee on the Joint Letter of the Five Communist and Workers' Parties ', *The Times*, 19 July 1968.

¹⁶ See ' Statement of the Communist and Workers' Parties of Socialist Countries, Bratislava ', *Pravda*, 4 Aug. 1968: *CDSP*, 20/31 (1968), pp. 4 f. Cf. Löwenthal, p. 20.

¹⁷ For German translation of the full text of the new Czechoslovak-Rumanian treaty of friendship, co-operation, and mutual assistance, 16 Aug. 1968, see *Archiv der Gegenwart*, 17 Aug. 1968, C.14123. In his speech at the signing of the treaty, Dubcek *did* refer to developments in West Germany, but again in a carefully balanced fashion. He declared himself against the rise of militarism and revanchism in West Germany, and lent his support to the democratic forces in the country. Ibid. C.14124.

¹⁸ See the declaration adopted by the Politbureau of the Central Committee of the CPSU, 6 Aug. 1968, *Pravda*, 7 Aug. 1968: *CDSP*, 20/32 (1968), p. 13.

[19] See e.g. the positive assessment of events in Czechoslovakia by Chancellor Kiesinger on 2 Apr. 1968, *Bulletin*, 44 (1968), p. 354.

[20] Address to the Assembly of Western European Union, Paris, *DOSB*, 59/1533 (1968), p. 490.

[21] See e.g. Katzenbach's address at San Francisco, 9 Aug. 1968, *DOSB*, 59/1523 (1968), pp. 237–40; Secretary Rusk's statement at Bonn, 26 June 1968, and Deputy Under Secretary Charles Bohlen's speech at San Diego, Calif., 24 June 1968, both in *DOSB*, 59/1516 (1968), pp. 74 f. and 70–4, resp.

[22] Lecture in Vienna, 10 June 1968, reproduced in part in Hansjacob Stehle, ' Die Blockierte Ostpolitik ', *Die Zeit*, 6 Dec. 1968, and speech to the *Bundestag*, 20 June 1968, *Bulletin*, 77 (1968).

[23] See the editorial ' Strengthen Peace in Europe ', *Pravda*, 20 Sept. 1968: *CDSP*, 20/38 (1968), p. 13.

[24] S. Kovalev, ' On " peaceful " and non-peaceful counter-revolution ', *Pravda*, 11 Sept. 1968: *CDSP*, 20/37 (1968), pp. 11 f.

[25] See the editorial in *Trybuna Ludu*, 31 Aug. 1968; also Foreign Minister Otto Winzer's address to 9th Plenary Session of Central Committee of the SED, East Berlin, 22–25 Oct. 1968, *Aussenpolitische Korrespondenz* (East Berlin, GDR Ministry for Foreign Affairs), 44 (1968).

[26] See e.g. the interview given by Chancellor Kiesinger, 25 Aug. 1968, *Bulletin*, 104 (1968).

[27] See Foreign Minister Michel Debré's declaration to the French National Assembly, 2 Oct. 1968, *ND*, 3587–9 (1969), pp. 99–104; also address by Katzenbach, 16 Oct. 1968, cited in n. 20.

[28] For West German assertions about a new element of uncertainty in East–West relations introduced by the Soviet invasion of Czechoslovakia, see the interview with Brandt, 1 Sept. 1968, *Bulletin*, 108 (1968), p. 925, and also debate in the *Bundestag*, 26 Sept. 1968, *Bulletin*, 123 (1968), p. 1056. Katzenbach stated in his address of 16 Oct. 1968 that ' given the Russian sense of insecurity that was so much a factor in the invasion—we must ask whether this same insecurity could not some day lead the Soviets to take a more rash step.'

[29] See his statement at the National Press Club, Washington, 5 Sept. 1968, *USIS News Bulletin* (Stockholm, US Embassy), 60 (1968).

[30] See e.g. remarks by Helmut Schmidt, SPD leader in the *Bundestag*, during the debate on 26 Sept. 1968, *Bulletin*, 123 (1968), p. 1059.

[31] S. Kovalev, ' Sovereignty and the international duties of Socialist countries ', *Pravda*, 26 Sept. 1968: *Soviet News* (London, Soviet Embassy) 1 Oct. 1968. For Gromyko's address to the UN General Assembly see *GAOR*, 23rd sess., plen. mtg 1679, 3 Oct. 1968. For an analysis of earlier Soviet or Moscow-inspired pronouncements containing elements of the same doctrine, see T. Schweisfurth, ' Moskauer Doktrin und sozialistischer Internationalismus ', *Aussenpolitik*, 19/12 (1968), pp. 710–19.

[32] Kovalev, ' Sovereignty and the international duties of Socialist countries '.

[33] In Feb. 1918 Lenin stated that ' no Marxist without renouncing the principles of Marxism and of socialism generally, can deny that the interests of socialism are higher than the interests of the right of nations to self-determination ', *Collected Works*, 4th ed. (London, 1964), vol. 26, p. 449.

[34] cf. Harlan Cleveland, ' NATO after the Invasion ', *Foreign Affairs*, 47/2 (1968–9), p. 253.

[35] Final communiqué of the ministerial meeting of NATO Council, Brussels, Nov. 1968, para. 6; *NATO Letter*, 16/12 (1968), p. 12.

[36] See reports by Hans Ulrich Kempski in *Süddeutsche Zeitung*, 18 Nov. 1968, Charles Douglas-Home in *The Times*, 19 Nov. 1968, and Drew Middleton in *The New York Times*, 17 Nov. 1968. See also report of TV interview with Dean Rusk, 1 Dec. 1968, when in response to a question about his speech at the Brussels NATO meeting he said, *inter alia*: ' I did not wish, at least publicly, to get into discussions about individual countries that would create problems for those individual countries. But when I was talking privately among foreign ministers—I am not a village idiot—when we talk about the possibility of further Soviet moves of the sort that were taken in Czechoslovakia, we talked about some of the specific possibilities.' *USIS News Bulletin* (Stockholm, US Embassy), 75 (1968).

[37] See Gromyko's speech, 27 June 1968, to Supreme Soviet, *Pravda*, 28 June 1968: *CDSP*, 20/28 (1968), pp. 11–16; and to UN General Assembly, 3 Oct. 1968, *GAOR*, 23rd sess., plen. mtg 1679.

[38] ' Encouraging the Rule of Reason in Eastern Europe and the Middle East ', address to 125th anniversary meeting of B'nai B-rith, Washington, 10 Sept. 1968, *DOSB*, 59/1528 (1968), pp. 345–9.

[39] See the government declaration of 21 Aug. 1968, *Bulletin*, 102 (1968), p. 873; interview with Chancellor Kiesinger, 25 Aug. 1968, *Bulletin*, 104 (1968), p. 889; and declaration by Foreign Minister Brandt, 22 Aug. 1968, *Bulletin*, 103 (1968), p. 884.

[40] See the recommendation adopted by NATO Assembly at its 14th annual conference, Brussels, 11–15 Nov. 1968, *NATO Letter*, 16/12 (1968), pp. 22–4.

[41] See above, p. 16.

[42] Address to the British Atlantic Committee, 6 Nov. 1968, mimeograph (London, Ministry of Defence), paras. 27 and 28. The address is reprinted in part in *NATO Letter*, 17/1 (1969), pp. 26–28.

[43] A phrase used by de Gaulle at press conference, 4 Feb. 1965, La documentation française, *Articles et Documents*, 0.1645 (1965), ' Textes du Jour ', pp. 4–6: English translation, *Speeches*, no. 216. See above, p. 11.

[44] Press conference, 9 Sept. 1968, *ND*, 3587–9 (1969), pp. 59–61, and *The Times*, 10 Sept. 1968.

[45] Ibid.

[46] Foreign Minister Debré's declaration to the National Assembly, 2 Oct. 1968, *ND*, 3587–9 (1969), pp. 99–104.

[47] See Debré's speech to the National Assembly, 7 Nov. 1968, *ND*, 3587–9 (1969), pp. 149–61, and esp. 157–9.

[48] See the Bonn government's declaration announced to the *Bundestag* by Kiesinger on 25 Sept. 1968, *Bulletin*, 121 (1968), pp. 1037 ff.

[49] Brandt's statement to the *Bundestag*, 26 Sept. 1968, *Bulletin*, 123 (1968), p. 1062.

[50] Ibid. p. 1068.

[51] On the domestic determinants of this new turn in the *Deutschlandpolitik* of the Grand Coalition, see Peter Bender, ' Entspannung oder Sicherheit ? ', *Der Monat*, 20/242 (1968), pp. 5–9. For a perceptive analysis of Bonn's policy on intra-German relations up to the invasion of Czechoslovakia, see Karl Kaiser, *German Foreign Policy in Transition* (1968), pp. 108 ff.

[52] Brandt's speech to the *Bundestag*, 26 Sept. 1968, *Bulletin*, 123 (1968), p. 1064. Almost the same phrase was used on 25 Oct. 1968 by Gerhard Jahn, *Parlamentarischer Staatssekretär* in the Foreign Ministry, in a speech at Bad Godesberg, *Bulletin*, 140 (1968), p. 1226.

[53] Kiesinger gave an account of his conversation with Tsarapkin in his speech to the *Bundestag* on 25 Sept. 1968, *Bulletin*, 121 (1968), p. 1038.

[54] See Kiesinger's address of 6 Oct. 1968, *Bulletin*, 126 (1968), pp. 1085 ff., the government declaration of 16 Oct. 1968, *Bulletin*, 132 (1968), pp. 1141 f., and article by Herbert Wehner, Minister for All-German Affairs, ' Die Moskauer Doktrin und die internationale Sicherheit ', *Harburger Anzeiger und Nachrichten*, 9 Oct. 1968, reprinted in *Bulletin*, 130 (1968), p. 1123.

[55] See Wehner ibid.; also the speech of *Parlamentarischer Staatssekretär* Gerhard Jahn, 25 Oct. 1968, *Bulletin*, 140 (1968), p. 1226.

[56] cf. address by the Minister of Economics, Karl Schiller, 27 Sept. 1968, *Bulletin*, 125 (1968), pp. 1077 ff. He stressed that the USSR and the whole COMECON area would profit from intensified participation in the international division of labour, and that restrictions must inevitably limit the growth rate of the country or countries affected.

[57] See above, p. 90.

[58] According to the official UN record, Gromyko said, ' The Soviet Union actively cooperates with European states interested in a European *détente*, in a stronger European security, in improving and promoting relations of mutual benefit between the states of East and of West of that Continent. *These aims are facilitated by the development of bilateral relations. Today, too, the Soviet Union advocates the continuation and extension of all such useful work.*' (My italics.) *GAOR*, 23rd sess., plen. mtg 1679, 3 Oct. 1968. The italicized sentences did not appear in *Pravda*, 4 Oct. 1968.

[59] Address by Ulbricht in East Berlin, 7 Oct. 1968, *Aussenpolitische Korrespondenz*, 42 (1968).

[60] *Aussenpolitische Korrespondenz*, 44 (1968).

[61] Speech at Katowice, 11 Oct. 1968, *Daily News* (Warsaw, Polska Agencja Prasowa), 12 Oct. 1968.

[62] Ibid.; see also Gomulka's speech to 5th Party Congress of Polish United Workers' Party, 10 Nov. 1968, *Daily News*, 11 Nov. 1968.

[63] Speech of 11 Oct. 1968.

[64] *Documents, Articles and Information on Romania* (Agerpres), Suppl. no. 30, 30 Nov. 1968, p. 42.

[65] Ibid. present author's italics.

[66] Ibid. pp. 36 f.

[67] See his address to the Polish Party Congress, 12 Nov. 1968, and his speech the next day at the Warsaw Steel works, *Soviet News*, 19 Nov. 1968.

[68] Speech by Ceausescu, 29 Nov. 1968, as n. 64, p. 46.

[69] At the Political Academy to the Central Committee of the Hungarian Socialist Workers' Party, 11 Dec. 1968, quoted here from a mimeograph (unofficial translation) provided by the Hungarian Embassy, Stockholm.

[70] *Soviet News*, 18 Mar. 1969.

[71] My italics.

[72] See Brandt's speech at Hamburg, 7 May 1969, *Bulletin*, 59 (1969), pp. 498 f.

[73] See his speech at Warsaw, 17 May 1969, *Daily News*, 18 May 1969.

Chapter 4

[1] cf. Kaiser, *German Foreign Policy in Transition*, pp. 108 ff.; Melvin Croan, ' Bonn and Pankow ', *Survey*, 67 (1968), pp. 77–89, and ' Czechoslovakia, Ulbricht, and the German Problem ', *Problems of Communism*, 18/1 (1969), pp. 1–7.

[2] See Secretary McNamara's statement early in 1967 (as n. 99, ch. 1) p. 9; also Chancellor Kiesinger's speech, 9 Mar. 1967, *Bulletin*, 26 (1967), pp. 206 ff.

[3] See above, p. 23. On 29 Apr. 1967 Mr Harriman, US Ambassador at Large, said: ' The hope that the peoples of Western and Eastern Europe can work together for the common good can only be realized if both accept the existence of each other's political systems and avoid interference in each other's internal affairs.' Address at Harriman, N.Y., *DOSB*, 56/1457 (1967), p. 820.

[4] Mr Strauss's suggestion in 1966 to ' dismantle ' the communist regimes in Eastern Europe was an extreme position, see his *The Grand Design*, p. 18. A speech, 3 Sept. 1967, by his cabinet colleague, Kai-Uwe von Hassel, contained implications about a European settlement clearly at variance with the American position referred to in n. 3 above. On Polish-German relations, von Hassel said he could not see what would stand in the way of a settlement of unresolved issues if negotiations were conducted between ' a mature free Poland [' mündiges freies Polen '] and a reunited free Germany '. *Bulletin*, 94 (1967), pp. 801 ff.

[5] For an interesting discussion of the ambiguity in the Grand Coalition government's Eastern policy see Pierre Hassner, ' Change and Security in Europe ', Part I, *Adelphi Papers*, 45 (1968), p. 13.

[6] See above, pp. 33 ff.

[7] *Pravda*, 2 Apr. 1968: *CDSP*, 20/14 (1969), p. 28.

[8] See the testimony of George Ball in the summer of 1966, US Senate, Cttee on Foreign Relations, *United States Policy Toward Europe (and Related Matters)*, Hearings, 89th Congress, 2nd sess., pp. 340 f. See also the interview given by Mr Brosio, Secretary-General of NATO, ' Eine deutliche Warnung ', *Moderne Welt*, 9/1 (1968), p. 14, and the discussion of Strauss's ideas above, pp. 34 f.

[9] See Gerd Schmückle, ' " Big Lift " und Krisen-Streitmacht ', *Europa-Archiv*, 22/8 (1967), pp. 279–86.

[10] See above, p. 100.

[11] cf. Nerlich, p. 87.

[12] See reports of debates in the *Bundestag* on 6 and 7 Dec. 1967, *Süddeutsche Zeitung*, 7 and 8 Dec. 1967, resp. For a critique of West Germany's force structure in the light of the over-all requirements of a rational Western defence posture, see Gerhard Brandt, *Rüstung und Wirtschaft in der Bundesrepublik* (1966), *passim* and especially conclusions, pp. 340–8. See also Eberhard Schulz, *An Ulbricht führt kein Weg mehr vorbei* (1967), pp. 235 ff. Schulz argues that West Germany should withdraw from NATO's nuclear strike force for the sake of reconciliation with the East.

[13] cf. G. Brandt, pp. 342 ff.

[14] cf. P. Bender, *Zehn Gründe für die Anerkennung der DDR* (1968), pp. 37 ff.

[15] For suggestion of a similar approach and a plea for mutual recognition of certain ' essentials ' by both West and East Germany, see Kaiser, ' Deutsche Aussenpolitik nach der tschechoslowakischen Krise von 1968 ', *Europa-Archiv*, 24/10 (1969), p. 362. For the most detailed Western elaboration of arguments in favour of recognizing the GDR see Bender, *Zehn Gründe*.

[16] Melvin Croan rightly stressed this point when he asserted ' the validity of a much-tested theorem of intra-German politics: the impossibility of stabilizing one part of the divided nation without simultaneously threatening to destabilize the other part ', *Survey*, 67 (1968), p. 78.

[17] cf. Bender, *Zehn Gründe*, p. 89.

[18] This may suggest the advisability of some division of labour among the Western states in the management of relations with the East, already proposed by several observers—the US concentrating on the USSR, Western Europe on the other East European states. See Henry Kissinger, ' Das Dilemma der Macht ',

Die Zeit, 6 Dec. 1968, and Michel Tatu, ' La détente avec l'Est ', *Le Monde*, 24 May 1969.

[19] In the wake of the Czechoslovak crisis Anatole Shub asserted that ' it would be tragic if the West did not now realize the necessity of framing a qualitatively different response for the next " Czechoslovakia " or " Hungary " ' ; ' Lessons of Czechoslovakia ', *Foreign Affairs*, 47/2 (1968–9), p. 277. Yet if a similar disaster befell, say, Rumania, it is difficult to see how the West could, as he suggests, give the kind of assistance it gave Yugoslavia in 1948. And how could the necessary consensus be achieved in the West for a ' prompt, vigorous defence of the right to independence and non-alignment of communist as well as other sovereign states ' (ibid.) unless the security of Western Europe was patently threatened by developments in the East?

[20] Harriman's address of 29 Apr. 1967, *DOSB*, 56/1457 (1967), p. 820.

[21] See USSR memorandum to West Germany, 5 July 1968, *Europa-Archiv*, 23/16 (1968), pp. D378–86, also Ulbricht's New Year message, 31 Dec. 1967, *Neues Deutschland*, 1 Jan. 1968.

[22] For evidence that at least in 1964 the Polish government was prepared to view the recognition issue in these terms, see above, p. 74.

[23] On the ambiguous Soviet position with regard to the composition of a European security conference see above, p. 54.

[24] cf. conclusions of the study group of the Deutsche Gesellschaft für Auswärtige Politik, Bonn, ' Alternativen für Europa. Modelle möglicher Entwicklungen in den siebziger Jahren ', *Europa-Archiv*, 23/23 (1968), pp. 851–64.

[25] See above, p. 100.

[26] See report of Gromyko's visit to Ottawa, *The New York Times*, 4 Oct. 1969.

[27] J. Tobin, ' Raising the Incomes of the Poor ', in Kenneth Gordon, ed., *Agenda for the Nation* (1968), pp. 77 f.

[28] Ibid. p. 78.

[29] C. L. Schultze, ' Budget Alternatives after Vietnam ', ibid. p. 48.

[30] cf. George Liska, *Imperial America* (1967), *passim*.

[31] Henry A. Kissinger, ' Central Issues of American Foreign Policy ', in Gordon, ed., *Agenda for the Nation*, p. 614.

[32] cf. Erich Fromm, *The Revolution of Hope* (1968), pp. 33 ff.

[33] cf. Kissinger, as n. 31, p. 614.

[34] Hassner, p. 24; Alastair Buchan, ed., *Europe's Futures, Europe's Choices* (1969), pp. 161-2.

[35] For a stimulating discussion of possible future developments in the USSR, see symposium ' The Future of the Soviet Union ', with contributions by Michel Tatu, Wolfgang Leonhard, Malcolm Mackintosh, and Adam Ulam, *Interplay*, 2/10 (1969).

[36] Marshall Shulman, ' Relations with the Soviet Union ', in Gordon, ed., *Agenda for the Nation*, p. 391. See also Shulman's *Beyond the Cold War* (1966), p. 49.

[37] That is, in the sense used by Karl Deutsch, who coined the term. K. W. Deutsch and others, *Political Community and the North Atlantic Area* (1957), p. 5.

[38] Hassner, p. 23.

[39] Such confidence was expressed by Mr Brandt in an interview, *Weltwoche* (Zürich), 8 Jan. 1969, reprinted in *Bulletin*, 4 (1969), p. 33.

[40] cf. M. Tatu, ' The Future of Two Foreign Policies: The Soviet Union ', *Interplay*, 2/4 (1968), p. 7.

[41] cf. Merle Fainsod, ' Some Reflections on Soviet-American Relations ', *The American Political Science Review*, 42/4 (1968), p. 1096. See also Shulman, *Beyond the Cold War*, p. 44, where he has rightly emphasized that there is a large

political gap ' between the kind of pressures that the appetites for consumer goods create in Soviet society and those engendered by middle-class political forces in Western Europe and the United States '.

[42] These points can easily be traced back to the findings and ideas expounded in Fromm's *The Revolution of Hope*, especially ch. 5, ' Steps to the Humanization of Technological Society '.

[43] For evidence of these similarities in public mood in East and West, see Fromm, *passim*; R. Richta and others, *Civilizace na rozcesti; spolecenske a lidske souvislosti vedeckotechnicke revoluce* (Civilization at the cross-roads; social and human implications of the scientific and technological revolution), an interdisciplinary study published by the Czechoslovak Academy of Science (1967); A. D. Sakharov, ' Thoughts on Progress, Peaceful Co-existence, and Intellectual Freedom ', *The New York Times*, 22 July 1968.

BASIC DOCUMENTS

Czechoslovakia

Report of First Secretary Alexander Dubcek to the Plenary of the CPCS Central Committee, 1 Apr. 1968. *La documentation française, Notes et études documentaires*, 3532 (1968).

'The point of view of the Presidium of the Czechoslovak Communist Party Central Committee on the Joint Letter of the Five Communist and Workers' Parties', 18 July 1968. *The Times*, 19 July 1968.

France

President de Gaulle. Press conference, 4 Feb. 1965. *La documentation française, Articles et Documents*, 0.1645 (1965), 'Textes du Jour'.

—— Press conference, 9 Sept. 1968. *La documentation française, Notes et études documentaires*, 3587–9 (1969).

Federal Republic of Germany

Government declaration, 13 Dec. 1966. *Europa-Archiv*, 22/1 (1967).

Foreign Minister Willy Brandt. Address to the Council of Europe, 24 Jan. 1967. *Europa-Archiv*, 22/4 (1967).

Government declaration, 26 Sept. 1968. *Bulletin des Presse- und Informationsamtes der Bundesregierung*, 123 (1968).

German Democratic Republic

First Secretary Walter Ulbricht. Report to the 13th meeting of the SED, 15 Sept. 1966. *Die Deutsche Demokratische Republik, die Europäische Sicherheit und die Entspannung der Beziehungen zwischen beiden deutschen Staaten*. Berlin, Dietz Verlag, 1966.

—— New Year address, 31 Dec. 1967. *Neues Deutschland*, 1 Jan. 1969.

Hungary

Foreign Minister Janos Peter. Lecture at the Political Academy to the Central Committee of the Hungarian Socialist Workers' Party, 11 Dec. 1968. Mimeograph (unofficial translation), Stockholm, Hungarian Embassy.

Poland

First Secretary Wladyslaw Gomulka. Speech at Karlovy Vary, 24 Apr. 1967. *Information Bulletin*, 8 (1967). Prague, Peace and Socialism Publishers.

—— Address at Katowice, 11 Oct. 1968. *Daily News*, 12 Oct. 1968. Warsaw, Polska Agencja Prasowa.

—— Speech at Warsaw, 17 May 1969. *Daily News*, 18 May 1969.

Rumania

General Secretary Nicolae Ceausescu. Speech on the occasion of the 45th anniversary of the Rumanian Communist Party, 7 May 1966. Bucharest, Agerpres.

—— Speech of 29 Nov. 1968. *Documents, Articles and Information on Romania*, supplement no. 30, 30 Nov. 1968. Bucharest, Agerpres.

USSR

First Secretary Leonid Brezhnev. Report of the CPSU Central Committee to the 23rd Congress of the CPSU, 29 Mar. 1966. *Pravda*, 30 Mar. 1966.

Resolution of the Central Committee of the CPSU, 10 Apr. 1968. *Pravda*, 11 Apr. 1968.

Foreign Minister Andrei Gromyko. Address to the United Nations General Assembly, 3 Oct. 1968. *GAOR*, 23rd sess., plen. mtg 1679.

UK

Minister of Defence Denis Healey. Speech to the House of Commons, 27 Feb. 1967. HC Deb., vol. 742, coll. 110 f.

USA

President Johnson. Address at New York, 7 Oct. 1966. *The Department of State Bulletin*, 55/1426 (1966).

Under Secretary of State Nicholas de B. Katzenbach. Address to the WEU Assembly, Paris, 16 Oct. 1968. *The Department of State Bulletin*, 59/1533 (1968).

Joint Eastern documents

' Declaration on the Strengthening of Peace and Security in Europe adopted by the Political Consultative Committee of the Warsaw Treaty Member States '. Bucharest, Agerpres, 5 July 1966.

' Statement by European Communist and Workers' Parties, Participants in the Conference at Karlovy Vary'. *Information Bulletin*, 9–10 (1967). Prague, Peace and Socialism Publishers.

Joint letter of the five allies to the Central Committee of the CPCS (so-called Warsaw Letter), 15 July 1968. *Pravda*, 18 July 1968.

Appeal of the WTO Political Consultative Committee to all European states, Budapest, 17 Mar. 1969. *Soviet News*, 18 Mar. 1969. London, Soviet Embassy.

Joint Western documents

Annex to the final communiqué of the NATO Council meeting in Luxembourg, 12–14 Dec. 1967, ' Future Tasks of the Alliance ' (so-called Harmel Report). *The Department of State Bulletin*, 58/1489 (1968).

Final Communiqué of the Ministerial Meeting of the NATO Council, Brussels, 15–16 Nov. 1968. *NATO Letter*, 16/12 (1968).

SELECT BIBLIOGRAPHY

Balfour, Michael. *West Germany*. London, 1968.

Ball, George W. *The discipline of power*. London, 1968.

Baring, Arnulf. *Aussenpolitik in Adenauers Kanzlerdemokratie; Bonns Beitrag zur Europäischen Verteidigungsgemeinschaft*. Munich, 1969.

Bender, Peter. 'Entspannung oder Sicherheit?' *Der Monat*, 20/242 (1968).

—— *Zehn Gründe für die Anerkennung der DDR*. Frankfurt-am-Main, 1968.

Berner, Wolfgang. 'Die Karlsbader Konferenz der Kommunistischen Parteien Europas'. *Berichte des Bundesinstituts für ostwissenschaftlichen und internationale Studien*, 30 (1967).

Birnbaum, Immanuel. *Entzweite Nachbarn: Deutsche Politik in Osteuropa*. Frankfurt-am-Main, 1968.

Birnbaum, Karl E. 'The nordic countries and European security'. *Cooperation and Conflict*, 3/1 (1968).

Brandt, Gerhard. *Rüstung und Wirtschaft in der Bundesrepublik*. Berlin, 1966. (Georg Picht, ed., Studien zur Politischen und gesellschaftlichen Situation der Bundeswehr, 3rd series.)

Brandt, Willy. *Aussenpolitik, Deutschlandpolitik, Europapolitik*. Berlin, 1968.

—— 'Entspannungspolitik mit langem Atem'. *Aussenpolitik*, 18/8 (1967). This article has appeared in English as '*Détente* over the long haul'. *Survival*, 9/10 (1967).

—— *Friedenspolitik in Europa*. Frankfurt-am-Main, 1968.

Brown, J. F. The New Eastern Europe. London, 1966.

Brzezinski, Zbigniew. *Alternative to partition; for a broader conception of America's role in Europe*. New York, 1965.

—— 'The framework of East–West reconciliation'. *Foreign Affairs*, 46/2 (1967/8).

Buchan, Alastair, ed. *Europe's futures, Europe's choices; models of Western Europe in the 1970s*. London, 1969.

Byrnes, R. F., ed. *The United States and Eastern Europe*. Englewood Cliffs, N.J., 1967.

Campbell, John C. *American policy toward Eastern Europe; the choice ahead*. Minneapolis, 1965.

Chalfont, Lord. 'Value of observation posts in NATO and Warsaw pact areas'. *European Review*, 16/4 (1966).

Cleveland, Harlan. 'NATO after the invasion'. *Foreign Affairs*, 47/2 (1968/9).

Croan, Melvin. 'Bonn and Pankow. Intra-German politics'. *Survey*, 67 (1968).

—— 'Czechoslovakia, Ulbricht, and the German Problem'. *Problems of Communism*, 18/1 (1969).

Cromwell, William C., ed. *Political problems of Atlantic partnership; national perspectives*. Bruges, 1969.

Dallin, Alexander and Thomas B. Larson, eds. *Soviet politics since Khrushchev*. Englewood Cliffs, N.J., 1968.

Deutsch, Karl W. and others. *Political community and the North Atlantic area.* New Haven, Conn., 1966.

Deutsche Gesellschaft für Auswärtige Politik (Bonn). 'Alternativen für Europa. Modelle möglicher Entwicklungen in den siebziger Jahren'. *Europa-Archiv*, 23/23 (1968).

Eppler, Erhard. 'Die europäische Funktion der Deutschen'. *Die Zeit*, 27 Oct. 1967; reprinted in E. Eppler, *Spannungsfelder*, Stuttgart, 1968.

Fainsod, Merle, 'Some reflections on Soviet–American relations'. *The American Political Science Review*, 42/4 (1968).

Foster, William C. 'New directions in arms control and disarmament'. *Foreign Affairs*, 43/4 (1964/5).

Fromm, Erich. *The revolution of hope: toward a humanized technology.* New York, 1968.

Gamarnikow, Michael. 'Political patterns and economic reforms'. *Problems of Communism*, 18/2 (1969).

Hassel, Kai-Uwe von. *Verantwortung für die Freiheit; Auszüge aus Reden und Veröffentlichungen 1963–1964.* Boppard, 1965.

Hassner, Pierre. 'Change and security in Europe', Part I. *Adelphi Papers*, 45 (1968).

Hoffmann, Stanley. *Gulliver's troubles, or the setting of American foreign policy.* New York, 1968.

Kaiser, Karl. 'Deutsche Aussenpolitik nach der tschechoslowakischen Krise von 1968'. *Europa-Archiv*, 24/10 (1969).

—— *German foreign policy in transition; Bonn between East and West.* London, 1968.

Kegel, Gerhard. 'Zur Deutschlandpolitik der beiden Deutschlands'. *Einheit*, 28/6 (1968).

Kissinger, Henry A. 'Central issues of American foreign policy', in Kenneth Gordon, ed., *Agenda for the nation.* New York, 1968.

—— 'Das Dilemma der Macht'. *Die Zeit*, 6 Dec. 1968.

Kitzinger, Uwe. *The politics and economics of European integration.* New York, 1963.

Kotyk, Vaclav. 'Problems of East–West relations'. *Journal of International Affairs*, 22/1 (1968).

Kovalev, Sergei. 'On "peaceful" and non-peaceful counter-revolution'. *Pravda*, 11 Sept. 1968.

—— 'Sovereignty and the international duties of socialist countries'. *Pravda*, 26 Sept. 1968.

Kuby, Hans. 'German foreign, defence, and European policy'. *Journal of Common Market Studies*, 6/2 (1967/8).

Leonhard, Wolfgang and others. 'The future of the Soviet Union'. *Interplay*, 2/10 (1969).

Liska, George. *Imperial America: the international politics of primacy.* Baltimore, 1967.

Liska, Ladislav. 'On the problem of European security'. *International Relations* (Prague), 1967.

Löwenthal, Richard. 'The Sparrow in the Cage'. *Problems of Communism* 17/6 (1968).

Mackintosh, Malcolm. 'The evolution of the Warsaw pact'. *Adelphi Papers*, 58, (1969).

Nerlich, Uwe. *Europäische Sicherheit der 70er Jahre*. Eggenberg, Stiftung Wissenschaft und Politik, Report No. AZ/147, 1968.

Passeron, André. *De Gaulle parle 1962–1966*. Paris, 1966.

Polyanov, N. and others. 'Problems of International Security' (in Russian). *Kommunist*, 43/11 (1966).

Remington, Robin Alison. 'The changing Soviet perception of the Warsaw pact.' Unpublished MS, November 1967, Center for International Studies, Massachusetts Institute of Technology, ref. no. C/67–24.

Richta, R. and others. *Civilizace na rozcesti; spolecenske a lidske souvislosti vedeckotechnicke revoluce*. Prague, Svoboda, 1967.

Rosecrance, Richard N. *Defense of the realm; British strategy in the nuclear epoch*. New York, 1968.

Sakharov, A. D. 'Thoughts on progress, peaceful co-existence, and intellectual freedom'. *The New York Times*, 22 July 1968.

Schelling, Thomas C. *Arms and influence*. New Haven, Conn., 1966.

Schmückle, Gerd. ' "Big Lift" und Krisen-Streitmacht'. *Europa-Archiv*, 22/8 (1967).

Schultze, Charles L. 'Budget alternatives after Vietnam', in Kenneth Gordon, ed., *Agenda for the nation*. New York, 1968.

Schulz, Eberhard. *An Ulbricht führt kein Weg mehr vorbei: Provozierende Thesen zur deutschen Frage*. Hamburg, 1967.

Schweisfurth, T. 'Moskauer Doktrin und sozialistischer Internationalismus'. *Aussenpolitik*, 19/12 (1968).

Shub, Anatole. 'Lessons of Czechoslovakia'. *Foreign Affairs*, 47/2 (1968/9).

Shulman, Marshall D. *Beyond the cold war*. New Haven, Conn., 1966.

—— ' "Europe" versus "détente"?' *Foreign Affairs*, 45/3 (1966/7).

—— 'Recent Soviet foreign policy: some patterns in retrospect'. *Journal of International Affairs*, 22/1 (1968).

—— 'Relations with the Soviet Union', in Kenneth Gordon, ed., *Agenda for the nation*. New York, 1968.

Stehle, Hansjakob. 'Wandel in Polen?' *Die Zeit*, 17 Nov. 1967.

Strauss, Franz Josef. *The Grand Design*. New York, 1966.

—— *Herausforderung und Antwort; Ein Programm für Europa*. Stuttgart, 1968.

Tatu, Michel. 'La détente avec l'Est; un slogan ou une politique?' *Le Monde*, 24 May 1969.

—— 'The future of two foreign policies; the Soviet Union'. *Interplay*, 2/4 (1968).

Tobin, James. 'Raising the incomes of the poor', in Kenneth Gordon, ed., *Agenda for the nation*. New York, 1968.

Tomashevsky, D. 'The USSR and the capitalist world'. *International Affairs* (Moscow), 13/3 (1966).

Ulam, Adam B. *Expansion and coexistence: the history of Soviet foreign policy 1917–1967*. London, 1968.

Vernant, Jacques. 'Après la conférence de presse 4 février'. *Revue de défense nationale*, 21/4 (1965).

Vetter, Gottfried, 'Zur Entwicklung der innerdeutschen Beziehungen'. *Europa-Archiv*, 23/9 (1968).

Wettig, Gerhard. 'Die europäische Sicherheit in der Politik des Ostblocks 1966'. *Osteuropa*, 17, 2–3 (1967).

—— 'Moskau und die Grosse Koalition in Bonn'. *Aus Politik und Zeitgeschichte*, supplement to *Das Parlament*, 6 Mar. 1968.

Windsor, Philip. 'NATO and European *détente*'. *The World Today*, 23/9 (1967).

——, and Adam Roberts. *Czechoslovakia 1968; reform, repression, and resistance*. London, 1969.

BOOKS WRITTEN UNDER THE AUSPICES
OF THE CENTER FOR INTERNATIONAL AFFAIRS
HARVARD UNIVERSITY

ECONOMIC AND POLITICAL DEVELOPMENT

United States Manufacturing in Brazil, by Lincoln Gordon and Engelbert L. Grommers, 1962. Harvard Business School.

The Economy of Cyprus, by A. J. Meyer, with Simos Vassiliou, 1962 (jointly with the Center for Middle Eastern Studies). Harvard University Press.

Entrepreneurs of Lebanon, by Yusif A. Sayigh, 1962 (jointly with the Center for Middle Eastern Studies). Harvard University Press.

Somali Nationalism, by Saadia Touval, 1963. Harvard University Press.

The Dilemma of Mexico's Development, by Raymond Vernon, 1963. Harvard University Press.

Africans on the Land, by Montague Yudelman, 1964. Harvard University Press.

People and Policy in the Middle East, by Max Weston Thornburg, 1964. Norton.

Foreign Aid and Foreign Policy, by Edward S. Mason, 1964 (jointly with the Council on Foreign Relations). Harper & Row.

Public Policy and Private Enterprise in Mexico, edited by Raymond Vernon, 1964. Harvard University Press.

The Rise of Nationalism in Central Africa, by Robert I. Rotberg, 1965. Harvard University Press.

Pan-Africanism and East African Integration, by Joseph S. Nye, Jr., 1965. Harvard University Press.

Political Change in a West African State, by Martin L. Kilson, 1966. Harvard University Press.

Planning without Facts: Lessons in Resource Allocation from Nigeria's Development, by Wolfgang F. Stolper, 1966. Harvard University Press.

Export Instability and Economic Development, by Alasdair I. MacBean, 1966. Harvard University Press.

Africa and United States Policy, by Rupert Emerson, 1967. Prentice-Hall.

Elites in Latin America, edited by Seymour M. Lipset and Aldo Solari, 1967. Oxford University Press.

Student Politics, edited by Seymour M. Lipset, 1967. Basic Books.

Pakistan's Development, by Gustav F. Papanek, 1967. Harvard University Press.

Strike a Blow and Die: A Narrative of Race Relations in Colonial Africa, by George Simeon Mwase. Edited and introduced by Robert I. Rotberg, 1967. Harvard University Press.

Party Systems and Voter Alignments, edited by Seymour M. Lipset and Stein Rokkan, 1967. Free Press.

Agrarian Socialism, by Seymour M. Lipset, revised edition, 1968. Doubleday Anchor.

Aid, Influence, and Foreign Policy, by Joan M. Nelson, 1968. Macmillan.

International Regionalism, by Joseph S. Nye, Jr., 1968. Little, Brown & Co.

152

Revolution and Counterrevolution, by Seymour M. Lipset, 1968. Basic Books.
Development Policy; Theory and Practice, edited by Gustav F. Papanek, 1968. Harvard University Press.
Political Order in Changing Societies, by Samuel P. Huntington, 1968. Yale University Press.
Korea: The Politics of the Vortex, by Gregory Henderson, 1968. Harvard University Press.
Political Development in Latin America, by Martin Needler, 1968. Random House.
The Precarious Republic, by Michael Hudson, 1968. Random House.
The Brazilian Capital Goods Industry, 1929–1964, by Nathaniel H. Leff, 1968. Harvard University Press.
Economic Policy-Making and Development in Brazil, 1947–1964, by Nathaniel H. Leff, 1968. Wiley.
Taxation and Development: Lessons from Colombian Experience, by Richard M. Bird, 1969. Harvard University Press.
East Africa and the Orient, edited by Robert I. Rotberg, 1969. Oxford University Press.
Agricultural Development in India's District: The Intensive Agricultural Districts Programme, by Dorris D. Brown, forthcoming from Harvard University Press.
Lord and Peasant in Peru, by F. LaMond Tullis, forthcoming from Harvard University Press.
Korean Development: The Interplay of Politics and Economics, by David C. Cole and Princeton N. Lyman, forthcoming from Harvard University Press.
Peasant Mobilization and Agrarian Reform in Venezuela, by John D. Powell, forthcoming from Harvard University Press.
Development Policy: The Pakistan Experience, edited by Walter P. Falcon and Gustav F. Papanek, forthcoming from Harvard University Press.

POLITICAL–MILITARY POLICY AND ARMS CONTROL.
The Necessity for Choice, by Henry A. Kissinger, 1961. Harper.
Strategy and Arms Control, by Thomas C. Schelling and Morton H. Halperin, 1961. Twentieth Century Fund.
Limited War in the Nuclear Age, by Morton H. Halperin, 1963. Wiley.
The Arms Debate, by Robert A. Levine, 1963. Harvard University Press.
Counterinsurgency Warfare, by David Galula, 1964. Praeger.
How Nations Negotiate, by Fred Charles Iklé, 1964. Harper & Row.
China and the Bomb, by Morton H. Halperin, 1965 (jointly with the East Asia Research Center). Praeger.
Communist China and Arms Control, by Morton H. Halperin and Dwight H. Perkins, 1965 (jointly with the East Asia Research Center). Praeger.
Problems of National Strategy, edited by Henry A. Kissinger, 1965. Praeger.
Deterrence before Hiroshima, by George H. Quester, 1966. Wiley.
Containing the Arms Race, by Jeremy J. Stone, 1966. M.I.T. Press.
Germany and the Atlantic Alliance, by James L. Richardson, 1966. Harvard University Press.

Arms and Influence, by Thomas C. Schelling, 1966. Yale University Press.
Contemporary Military Strategy, by Morton H. Halperin, 1967. Little, Brown & Co.
Sino-Soviet Relations and Arms Control, edited by Morton H. Halperin, 1967 (jointly with the East Asia Research Center). M.I.T. Press.
The TFX Tangle: McNamara and the Military, by Robert J. Art, 1968. Little, Brown & Co.
The Politics of Nonviolent Action, by Gene Sharp, 1970. The Pilgrim Press.

ATLANTIC STUDIES AND THE COMMUNIST BLOC

The Soviet Bloc, by Zbigniew K. Brzezinski 1960 (jointly with the Russian Research Center). Harvard University Press. Revised edition, 1967.
Rift and Revolt in Hungary, by Ferenc A. Vah, 1961. Harvard University Press.
Communist China 1955–1959: Policy Documents with Analysis, with a Foreword by Robert R. Bowie and John K. Fairbank, 1962 (jointly with the East Asia Research Center). Harvard University Press.
In Search of France, by Stanley Hoffmann *et al.*, 1963. Harvard University Press.
Shaping the Future, by Robert R. Bowie, 1964. Columbia University Press.
Democracy in Germany, by Fritz Erler, 1965 (Jodidi Lectures). Harvard University Press.
The Troubled Partnership, by Henry A. Kissinger, 1965 (jointly with the Council on Foreign Relations). McGraw-Hill.
Foreign Policy and Democratic Politics, by Kenneth N. Waltz, 1967 (jointly with the Institute of War and Peace Studies, Columbia University). Little, Brown & Co.
Europe's Postwar Growth, by Charles P. Kindleberger, 1967. Harvard University Press.
The Rise and Decline of the Cold War, by Paul Seabury, 1967. Basic Books.
German Foreign Policy in Transition, by Karl Kaiser, 1968. Oxford University Press.
Peace in Europe, by Karl E. Birnbaum, 1970. Oxford University Press.

OCCASIONAL PAPERS PUBLISHED BY
THE CENTER FOR INTERNATIONAL AFFAIRS

1. *A Plan for Planning: The Need for a Better Method of Assisting Under-developed Countries on Their Economic Policies*, by Gustav F. Papanek, 1961. Out of print.
2. *The Flow of Resources from Rich to Poor*, by Alan D. Neale, 1961. 83 pp.
3. *Limited War: An Essay on the Development of the Theory and an Annotated Bibliography*, by Morton H. Halperin, 1962. Out of print.
4. *Reflections on the Failure of the First West Indian Federation*, by Hugh W. Springer, 1962. Out of print.
5. *On the Interaction of Opposing Forces under Possible Arms Agreements*, by Glenn A. Kent, 1963. 36 pp.
6. *Europe's Northern Cap and the Soviet Union*, by Nils Örvik, 1963. 64 pp.
7. *Civil Administration in the Punjab: An Analysis of a State Government in India*, by E. N. Mangat Rai, 1963. 82 pp.
8. *On the Appropriate Size of a Development Program*, by Edward S. Mason, 1964. 24 pp.
9. *Self-Determination Revisited in the Era of Decolonization*, by Rupert Emerson, 1964. 64 pp.
10. *The Planning and Execution of Economic Development in Southeast Asia*, by Clair Wilcox, 1965. 37 pp.
11. *Pan-Africanism in Action*, by Albert Tevoedjre, 1965. 88 pp.
12. *Is China Turning In?* by Morton H. Halperin, 1965. 34 pp.
13. *Economic Development in India and Pakistan*, by Edward S. Mason, 1966. 67 pp.
14. *The Role of the Military in Recent Turkish Politics*, by Ergun Özbudun, 1966. 54 pp.
15. *Economic Development and Individual Change: A Social-Psychological Study of the Comilla Experiment in Pakistan*, by Howard Schuman, 1967. 59 pp.
16. *A Select Bibliography on Students, Politics, and Higher Education*, by Philip G. Altbach, 1967. 54 pp.
17. *Europe's Political Puzzle: A Study of the Fouchet Negotiations and the 1963 Veto*, by Alessandro Silj, 1967. 178 pp.
18. *The Cap and the Straits: Problems of Nordic Security*, by Jan Klenberg, 1968. 19 pp.
19. *Cyprus: The Law and Politics of Civil Strife*, by Linda B. Miller, 1968. 97 pp.
20. *East and West Pakistan: A Problem in the Political Economy of Regional Planning*, by Md. Anisur Rahman, 1968. 38 pp.
21. *Internal War and International Systems: Perspectives on Method*, by George A. Kelly and Linda B. Miller, 1969. 40 pp.
22. *Migrants, Urban Poverty, and Instability in New Nations*, by Joan M. Nelson, 1969. 81 pp.

INDEX

Adenauer, Konrad, 27
Anti-imperialist front, 49, 53 f., 56 ff., 65, 68, 76
Arms control, 16 f., 21, 30 f., 35, 39 f., 42, 51, 58, 65 f., 69, 72–5, 110, 115, 126

Ball, George W., 21
Bashev, Ivan, 62
Berlin question, 1, 28, 40, 112, 114 f., 117
Brandt, Willy, 30, 31–5, 86, 94
Brezhnev, Leonid, 2, 46, 48 ff., 57, 60, 64, 66, 72, 82, 99; Brezhnev Doctrine, 4, 88 f., 94, 96 ff.
Brown, George, 16
Brzezinski, Zbigniew, 22, 24 f.
Bucharest Declaration (1966), *see under* East–West relation in Europe
Bulgaria: relations with Federal Republic of Germany, 62, 68

Ceausescu, Nicolae, 50 f., 61, 73, 97 ff.
China, People's Republic of, 17, 21, 37, 47, 125
Cleveland, Harlan, 20
Clifford, Clark, 87
COMECON (Council for Mutual Economic Aid), 121
Conflict control: US, 38, 104; Federal Republic of Germany, 39 f.; France, 40
Counter-revolution, 83, 86 f., 98
Couve de Murville, Maurice, 13
Cuban crisis, 1, 19, 23
Czechoslovakia, 45 ff., 79 ff.; invasion of, 2 f., 42, 84 f., 105, 122; relations with Federal Republic of Germany, 59 ff., 68 f., 80 f.; — with German Democratic Republic, 80 f.; — with Rumania, 84; Action Programme (adopted 5 Apr. 1968), 78, 81

Debré, Michel, 92
Dubcek, Alexander, 46, 73, 79 ff.

East–West relations in Europe, 1–4; views of France, 9, 38, 40; — of UK, 16 ff., 38 f.; — of US, 19–21, 37 ff., 85 ff.; — of Federal Republic of Germany, 28 f., 38 ff., 86; — of USSR, 48 ff., 61–4, 79, 82; — of Rumania, 50 ff.; improvement by means of bilateral relations, 10, 16, 20 f., 40, 42, 72, 75, 95, 116; Bucharest Declaration (1966), 52 f.; views of German Democratic Republic, 66 f.; — of Hungary, 67, 99 f.; — of Czechoslovakia, 79, 81

Europe, Eastern, 47, 105, 113 ff.
—Western, 104, 120 f.; integration of, 109, 121; views concerning integration: France, 11 f.; UK, 15, 91; US, 19, 26, 91; Federal Republic of Germany, 32 f., 34 f.

European co-operation, 109, 114, 121; views of France, 12; — of US, 24; — of Rumania, 51, 73, 75; — of WTO, 53 f.; — of USSR, 58, 72, 76 f.; — of Hungary, 75; — of Czechoslovakia, 80, 82

European Economic Community (EEC), 9, 15, 18, 109, 121, 124

European Security Conference (ESC), 54, 95, 100, 116 ff.

European security system, 53, 73, 75 f.; views of USSR, 2 f., 70 f.; — of France, 11; — of Federal Republic of Germany, 31 ff.; — of Rumania, 73

European settlement, 103 ff., 122–8; views of France, 10–12, 40 f., 91 f.; — of UK, 15 f., 18, 39; — of US, 22, 25–7, 38, 90; — of Federal Republic of Germany, 30–5, 39–41, 90, 94; — of USSR, 71 f., 90; — of German Democratic Republic, 72; — of Czechoslovakia, 73; — of Poland, 73; — of Rumania, 73; — of WTO, 75 f.

European *status quo*, 38 ff., 57, 62, 68, 70 f., 73 f., 94, 105, 107, 117 f.

United States of America—*continued*
— with Western Europe, 18 f.;
— with Eastern Europe, 23 f.;
— with German Democratic Republic, 24; role in Europe, 108 ff.;
views of US role in Europe held by
France, 10 f.; — by US, 26; — by
Federal Republic of Germany, 32;
— by USSR, 49, 57 f., 72; — by
WTO, 54; — by Poland, 56; — by
German Democratic Republic, 72

Vaculik, Ludvik, 83

Vietnam, conflict in, 2, 19, 26, 37, 48,
51 f., 64, 67, 120

Warsaw Letter of 15 Jul. 1968, 83 f.
Warsaw Treaty Organization (WTO),
32 f., 50 f., 53, 55, 68, 71, 74, 84, 87,
100, 115, 121; relations between
members, 2 f., 52, 86
Wehner, Herbert, 30

Yugoslavia, 65, 88f.